D0789920

Tableau Desktop Pocket Reference
Essential Features, Syntax, and Data Visualizations

Ryan Sleeper

Beijing · Boston · Farnham · Sebastopol · Tokyo

To Tableau and its community,
Thank you for making my career fulfilling and fun.

Tableau Desktop Pocket Reference

by Ryan Sleeper

Printed in Canada.

Published by O'Reilly Media, Inc., 1005 Gravenstein Highway North, Sebastopol, CA 95472.

O'Reilly books may be purchased for educational, business, or sales promotional use. Online editions are also available for most titles (*http://oreilly.com*). For more information, contact our corporate/institutional sales department: 800-998-9938 or *corporate@oreilly.com*.

Acquisitions Editor: Michelle Smith
Development Editor: Corbin Collins
Production Editor: Katherine Tozer
Copyeditor: Sharon Wilkey
Proofreader: Christina Edwards
Indexer: Ellen Troutman-Zaig
Interior Designer: David Futato
Cover Designer: Karen Montgomery
Illustrator: Kate Dullea

May 2021:   First Edition

Revision History for the First Edition

2021-04-20:   First Release

See   *http://oreilly.com/catalog/errata.csp?isbn=9781492093480*   for   release details.

978-1-492-09348-0

[MBP]

Table of Contents

Preface

The single most-common question I hear is, "What advice do you have for someone getting started with Tableau?" I've always said that Tableau is one of those tools that takes a day to learn but a lifetime to master. The book you're reading now covers all the topics I wish I knew the first day I opened Tableau Desktop over a decade ago.

While I've covered many of these topics before in my first book, *Practical Tableau,* I have completely rewritten every chapter from scratch to incorporate everything I've learned along the way. My hope is that you find this book to be a rock-solid foundation and reference during your own Tableau and visual analytics journey.

Conventions Used in This Book

The following typographical conventions are used in this book:

Italic

Indicates new terms, URLs, email addresses, filenames, and file extensions.

`Constant width`

Used for program listings, as well as within paragraphs to refer to program elements such as variable or function

names, databases, data types, environment variables, statements, and keywords.

`Constant width bold`
> Shows commands or other text that should be typed liter-
> ally by the user.

`Constant width italic`
> Shows text that should be replaced with user-supplied val-
> ues or by values determined by context.

Playfair Data TV

With a mission to create a comprehensive blended learning
environment, Playfair Data launched its own on-demand
Tableau training platform, Playfair Data TV (*https://oreil.ly/
bYBG2*). With more than 100 episodes covering many
approaches developed personally by the instructor, Playfair
Data TV is one of the largest and fastest-growing collections of
Tableau video tutorials available.

O'Reilly Online Learning

For more than 40 years, *O'Reilly
Media* has provided technology and
business training, knowledge, and
insight to help companies succeed.

Our unique network of experts and innovators share their
knowledge and expertise through books, articles, and our
online learning platform. O'Reilly's online learning platform
gives you on-demand access to live training courses, in-depth
learning paths, interactive coding environments, and a vast col-
lection of text and video from O'Reilly and 200+ other publish-
ers. For more information, visit *http://oreilly.com*.

How to Contact Us

Please address comments and questions concerning this book to the publisher:

O'Reilly Media, Inc.
1005 Gravenstein Highway North
Sebastopol, CA 95472
800-998-9938 (in the United States or Canada)
707-829-0515 (international or local)
707-829-0104 (fax)

We have a web page for this book, where we list errata, examples, and any additional information. You can access this page at *https://oreil.ly/tableau-pocket-ref*.

Email *bookquestions@oreilly.com* to comment or ask technical questions about this book.

For news and information about our books and courses, visit *http://oreilly.com*.

Find us on Facebook: *http://facebook.com/oreilly*

Follow us on Twitter: *http://twitter.com/oreillymedia*

Watch us on YouTube: *http://www.youtube.com/oreillymedia*

Acknowledgments

I would like to thank the following people who went above and beyond what was asked to improve the quality of this book:

Brandi Beals, Ethan Lang, and Ken Flerlage for your technical reviews and patience as I refined my thoughts. Corbin Collins for your editing and meticulous attention to detail. Jason Penrod for lending your design and user experience expertise to the figures in this book.

CHAPTER 1

Tableau's Product Ecosystem

The first thing to know as you're getting started is that you don't simply "download Tableau." Tableau is a *brand*—and under its brand umbrella, it provides a family of end-to-end, self-service analytics *products*, spanning data engineering to dashboard distribution. The choice of which product you download, use, or access comes down to your role within your organization, the permissions you have to access confidential company data, and/or the trust you have to share insights with others. This chapter covers Tableau's current product lineup, its licensing model, and version updates.

Tableau Products

Tableau Prep Builder is drag-and-drop data engineering software that allows you to connect to various data sources and prepare them for use with Tableau Desktop or other software programs. With Tableau Prep Builder, you can combine, clean, aggregate, and/or pivot data before either saving it locally or publishing it to a central repository for others to use.

Tableau Prep Conductor, included in Tableau's Data Management add-on, allows you to schedule and automate the data engineering *flows* that are developed within Tableau Prep Builder.

Tableau Desktop is drag-and-drop analytics and data visualization software. With Tableau Desktop, you can connect to a wide variety of data sources, explore data of all sizes, create ad hoc analyses on the fly, combine multiple elements into cohesive dashboards for easier consumption, share views with others, and much more. Tableau Desktop is the focus of this book.

Tableau Public is a free version of Tableau Desktop that allows you to connect to a limited number of data source types such as Microsoft Excel and create public analyses. The catch with Tableau Public being free is you must save your work to the public web, where anybody can see it, making it unsuitable for proprietary data. That being said, Tableau Public is a great option for practicing Tableau Desktop and analyzing data sources outside the office or nonprotected company data.

Tableau Server is a central repository, managed by your organization, that stores all published workbooks built in Tableau Desktop, shared data sources, and/or Tableau Prep workflows. With Tableau Server, you can grant access permissions to workbooks and data sources, schedule data refreshes, collaborate on analyses with commenting and email, and make web-based edits to content published from Tableau Desktop.

Tableau Online has nearly all the same functionality as Tableau Server but is hosted by Tableau itself.

Tableau Reader is a free desktop application that allows a user to view and interact with analyses saved as a packaged workbook from Tableau Desktop.

Tableau Mobile is a free mobile app that allows a user to view and interact with analyses published to Tableau Server or Tableau Online.

Tableau License Model

Tableau uses a license-based model (with the exception of its free Tableau Public product) that bundles several of its flagship products together. Depending on whether a user is a *Creator*, *Explorer*, or *Viewer* determines how they can access files, interact with views, collaborate on analyses, author new analyses, prepare data sources, and govern permissions (Figure 1-1).

	Creator	Explorer	Viewer
	TABLEAU DESKTOP TABLEAU PREP TABLEAU SERVER	TABLEAU SERVER	TAB FAU SERVER
ACCESS	✔	✔	✔
INTERACT	✔	✔	Limited
COLLABORATE	✔	✔	Limited
AUTHOR	Create & Publish	Edit & Publish	
PREPARE	✔		
GOVERN	Admin Privileges	Manage	

Figure 1-1. Tableau products and features by license type. Tableau Server is used to represent both Tableau Server and Tableau Online.

Tableau Version Updates

Tableau is on an aggressive release schedule and provides new product updates to its Prep products as frequently as every month, and the Desktop product as frequently as every three months. As of 2018, Tableau versions list the year first, followed by a period and the sequential release within that year (for example, 2021.3). It is important to know which version of Tableau your company uses so that features are as in sync as possible throughout the organization.

To keep an eye on Tableau's latest feature offerings, see its New Features page (*https://oreil.ly/rkpYh*) on the website. To download previous versions of Tableau products, see its Releases page (*https://oreil.ly/9LTJT*).

CHAPTER 2

Shaping Data

Before you open Tableau Desktop, it's important to know that an optimal "shape," or layout, of data rows and columns can help you get the most out of the software. In fact, failing to prepare a data source for use with Tableau is what I view as the single biggest barrier to its adoption. I've seen this play out several times in my career as a consultant, but it also happens to be part of my own personal story, so I will share it from my perspective.

I'll never forget the day I was introduced to Tableau. My boss at the time walked into the office where our company's three analysts worked and said, "I've heard of this tool, Tableau; can the three of you take a shot at migrating our existing reports to the new software?" Like most companies, we were doing our data reporting almost exclusively in Microsoft Excel.

We opened Tableau Desktop, and lucky for us, the very first type of file that Tableau offers to connect to (as you will see in the next chapter) is Microsoft Excel. So we connected to our existing Excel reports, thinking the process would work great and maybe we could even head to happy hour early. Unfortunately, Tableau misclassified all the fields, we didn't know how to drag and drop anything to create meaningful visualizations, everything seemed broken, and before long many of us reverted to the familiarity of Excel.

Common Data Layout

Consider the layout shown in Table 2-1, which may look like an existing Excel report created at your office.

Table 2-1. Common data layout for Microsoft Excel reports

Quarterly Excel Report				
	Q1	Q2	Q3	Total
Sales	$$$	$$$	$$$	$$$$$
Profit	$$$	$$$	$$$	$$$$$
Profit Ratio	%%	%%	%%	%%
Quantity	###	###	###	#####

Understandably, Table 2-1 has been laid out in a way that makes it easy for a stakeholder to consume. For example, a title at the top explains what's in the table, date columns go from left to right to show trending, a computed ratio divides profit by sales (profit ratio) each quarter, and the Total column at the far right shows where we end up.

WARNING

Many of the features that make it easier for our stakeholders to consume a report in Excel make a table problematic in terms of the way Tableau interprets the data source and allows us to analyze it.

Ideal Data Layout

Unless you are planning to use Tableau only to re-create text table views, I highly recommend that you shape your data source like Table 2-2.

Table 2-2. Optimal data layout
for use with Tableau Desktop

Date	Sales	Profit	Quantity
1/1/2024	$$$	$$$	###
4/1/2024	$$$	$$$	###
7/1/2024	$$$	$$$	###

Note the changes I've made between the first and second tables:

- Removed the report title from the first row
- Pivoted my date fields from columns to rows
- Unpivoted my Sales, Profit, and Quantity fields from rows to columns
- Changed the data type of my date field from String (such as Q1, Q2, Q3) to Date (1/1/2024 and so on)
- Removed the Total column on the right
- Removed the Profit Ratio field, which will instead be aggregated in Tableau via a calculated field (see Chapter 11)

This is called a *tidy* data format: each column header is a *variable* in the data, and each row after that is a *record*. When data is in this format, each row becomes a combination of the column headers; this is what helps you slice and dice data in Tableau.

This tidy format helps Tableau not only know what fields are in your data and assign a data type to each column, but also classify each field as a dimension or measure and as discrete or continuous (discussed in Chapters 5 and 6, respectively).

How to Reshape Data

Tableau Desktop comes with features to help you reshape existing Excel reports into a tidy format for use with Tableau. If you connect to a data source that Tableau recognizes as not in the optimal format for analysis, you will see an option to Use Data Interpreter (Figure 2-1). When you toggle this feature on, Tableau will attempt to remove extra rows at the top, such as the title, which prevent Tableau from knowing which fields are represented in each column.

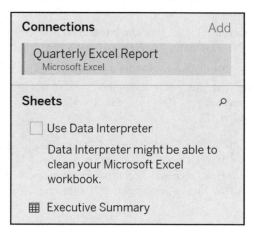

Figure 2-1. Tableau's Data Interpreter feature upon connecting to a data source

You can also hide unwanted columns, such as totals that will be aggregated later during analysis, by hovering over the unwanted column, clicking the down arrow that appears in the column's top-right corner, and choosing Hide, as shown in Figure 2-2.

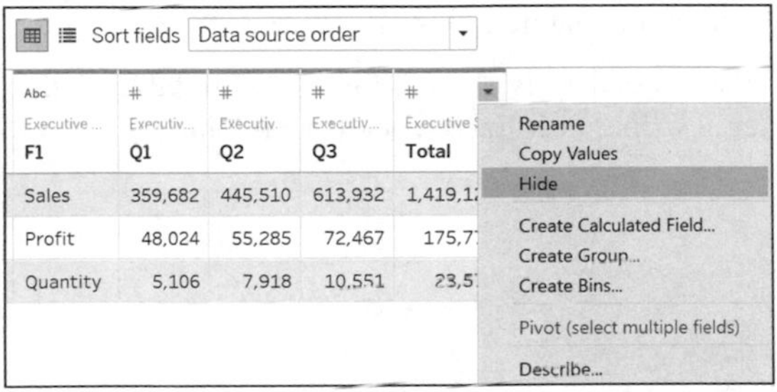

Figure 2-2. Hiding an unwanted column when connecting to a data source in Tableau Desktop

The last tasks needed to convert this data source into a tidy format would be to pivot the quarter fields from columns to rows and unpivot the field names from rows to columns. You can do a *pivot* in Tableau Desktop by selecting multiple columns in the connection interface, clicking the down arrow that appears when hovering over any of the columns, and selecting Pivot, as shown in Figure 2-3.

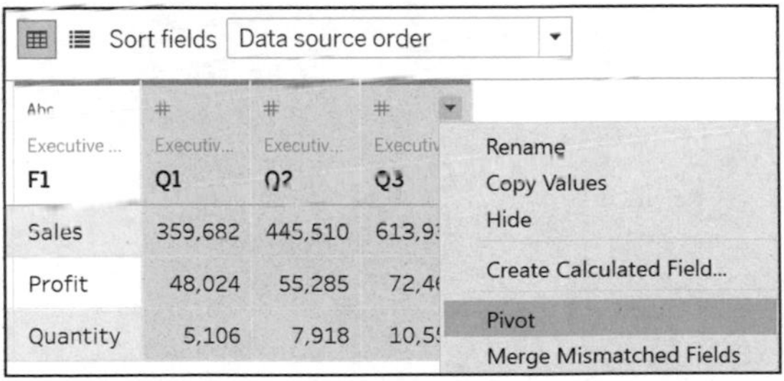

Figure 2-3. Pivoting columns to rows in Tableau Desktop

Currently, Tableau Desktop has no option to *unpivot* the field names from rows to columns. For this reason, I recommend that you shape data for use in Tableau Desktop in a tool designed specifically for that purpose, such as Tableau Prep Builder, which comes with the Creator license described in Chapter 1. Tableau Prep Builder can perform all the operations described in this chapter, plus much more.

Now that your data is shaped for use with Tableau, the next chapter describes how to connect to a data source.

CHAPTER 3

Connecting to Data

Upon opening Tableau for the first time, you're presented with the Connect pane on the left side of the screen, where you can connect to various types of data sources. The data connections are split into four areas:

Search for Data

Allows you to connect to data sources shared to Tableau Server or Tableau Online as published data sources (discussed in Chapter 14).

To a File

Allows you to connect to flat data files such as Excel workbooks, text files (including comma-separated files), and JavaScript Object Notation (JSON) files.

To a Server

Allows you to connect to data hosted on a server such as Microsoft SQL Server, Oracle, Amazon Redshift, and many more—which you can access by clicking the More option.

Saved Data Sources

These data sources are shared to your Tableau repository for easy access. By default, this section contains two sample data sources that you can use for Tableau practice and for following along with this book.

As of this writing, Tableau Desktop has 83 native data connections in the Microsoft Windows version of the software—plus the ability to connect to third-party web data connectors, Java Database Connectivity (JDBC), and Open Database Connectivity (ODBC). Slightly fewer connections are available in the Mac version of Tableau Desktop. To get started analyzing a data source, click its connection type from the Connect pane, as shown in Figure 3-1.

To follow the examples in this book, you can click Sample – Superstore near the bottom of the Connect pane. Saved data sources are unique in that they immediately bring you into the Authoring interface. We'll discuss this interface in more detail in coming chapters, but to see what typically happens when you access a data source for the first time, let's connect to an unsaved version of the Sample – Superstore data source.

To connect to the unsaved version from the Connect pane, click Microsoft Excel (under To a File) and then navigate to Documents > My Tableau Repository > Datasources, and choose the version number you're using. From here, click the region folder relevant to your location (such as *en_US-US*) and you will see the Sample – Superstore Excel file. Double-click the file to access the Data Source interface (Figure 3-2), where you can prepare the file for analysis.

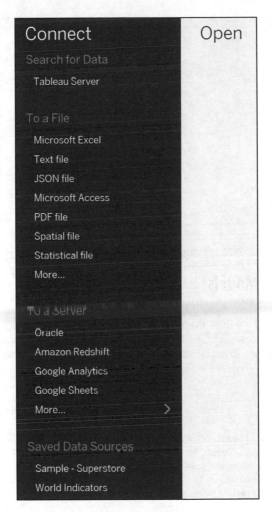

Figure 3-1. Tableau's Connect pane with native data connections

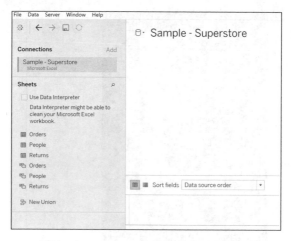

Figure 3-2. Tableau's Data Source interface

Data Models

Tableau interprets this Excel workbook as a database, and the three tabs within the workbook as database tables. I point this out because Tableau interprets server-based data sources the same way, so you'll see something similar when connecting to the data sources listed under To a Server on the Connect pane.

TIP

Don't be confused by seeing two occurrences of the Orders, People, and Returns options in this interface! The first three are the full tables, while the second set are Excel *named ranges*. In the following examples, we'll always connect to the Orders and Returns tables.

Tableau provides three types of table connections:

Single tables

These are the simplest and allow you to begin analyzing a single table by left-clicking and dragging the table name from the left pane to the interface label "Drag tables here." This option may be all you need, particularly if you've prepared a data source in a tool such as Tableau Prep before connecting here in Tableau Desktop.

Multiple tables (using Tableau's data model)

Tableau's data model introduces what Tableau calls a *logical layer* that combines tables by using *noodles*. This is the default way to connect multiple tables, as it combines the data in more intuitive ways and makes data preparation easier. This helps solve data challenges automatically, such as the need to deduplicate joined rows (you can read more about this in Chapter 50 of my book *Innovative Tableau* (O'Reilly, 2020).

Multiple tables (using joins and unions)

Prior to Tableau Desktop 2020.2, joins and unions were the default tactics for combining data in Tableau. As such, dragging a second table into the view would automatically create a join. Now, to access what Tableau calls the *physical layer*, you must double-click the primary table.

TIP

To learn more about Tableau's data model and how it differs from joins, see "The Tableau Data Model" (*https://oreil.ly/VvYLi*) on the Tableau website.

To begin an analysis, I will left-click and drag the Orders table from the Connections pane to the "Drag tables here" area. To add context to our analyses, I will also bring the Returns table into the data model by dragging it from the Connections pane, next to the Orders table. This automatically creates a relationship between the Orders and Returns tables in the logical layer on the Order ID field, as you can see in Figure 3-3.

In this case, Tableau was able to automatically create a relationship because both tables have a field with the same name. If Tableau does not automatically recognize a relationship, you can define one or more relationships in the Edit Relationship dialog that appears.

Figure 3-3. Tableau's Data model creating a relationship between the Orders and Returns tables from the Sample – Superstore data source

Live Data Connections Versus Data Extracts

As seen in the top-right corner of the Data Source interface (Figure 3-4), we can connect to a data source in two ways: Live or Extract.

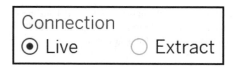

Figure 3-4. The Live and Extract radio buttons on Tableau's Data Source interface

Live data connections, the default, are exactly what they sound like: live connections to the underlying data source. This is the most secure option, as you are not creating copies of the data source or moving data around between systems; you are querying and visualizing the data from its hosted location. The drawback to this option is performance related. Since you are querying live, response time depends on factors including the size of the data source, the type of hardware, and the number of users sharing resources.

Extracts create a snapshot of the data by using Tableau's own Hyper data engine. These files, which end with the extension *.hyper*, are optimized for Tableau and will almost always perform faster than a live data connection. The drawbacks are that this option is less secure, as you're creating copies of a data source that can be distributed outside company servers and, because you're creating snapshots of a data source at a given point in time, you must refresh an extract to bring new data into the data source.

Data Source Versus Extract Filters

An optional preparation step you can do in the Data Source interface is to add a filter by clicking the Add button in the top-right corner, under Filters (Figure 3-5).

Figure 3-5. Add button for creating a Data Source filter

If you're using a live connection, the filters you add in this section create a *data source filter*.

If you're creating an extract, you'll see an Edit button appear next to the selected Extract radio button. If you click the Edit button and add filters in the dialog that appears, you're creating an *extract filter*.

These are the highest-level filters you can add in Tableau Desktop and the first processing that happens in Tableau's order of operations, discussed in more detail in Chapter 10.

Data Types

One more item you can update on this screen is the data type for each field in your dataset. In the top-left corner of each column, you'll see a blue or green icon (Figure 3-6) indicating the data type Tableau has assigned to each field.

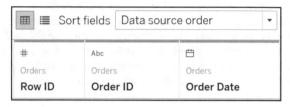

Figure 3-6. Data types in Tableau Desktop

It's important to understand data types because they often determine how data sources can be combined, which fields can be used within calculated fields, and what kind of chart types you can make. For example, you can't add an integer to a string in a calculation or make a map out of dates. The seven data types used in Tableau are as follows:

- Number (decimal)
- Number (whole)
- Date & Time
- Date
- String (i.e., text)
- Boolean (true or false)
- Geographic Role (i.e., latitude and longitude)

These classifications are correct most of the time, but these icons can be helpful in determining whether your dataset is optimized for your analyses. If you ever need to change a data type classification, click the data type icon and make a different selection (Figure 3-7).

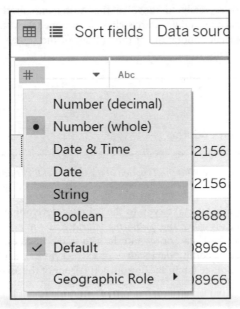

Figure 3-7. Changing a data type classification in Tableau Desktop

You can do a few additional data preparation tasks on this screen, but they are beyond the scope of this book. You can access them by clicking the down arrow that appears in the top-right corner of a column upon hovering.

TIP

For more information on preparing a data source for use with Tableau, I suggest reading Chapter 3 of my book *Practical Tableau* (O'Reilly, 2018) or for a thorough deep dive, *Tableau Prep: Up & Running* by Carl Allchin (O'Reilly, 2020).

Once you're ready to move to the Authoring interface and begin analyzing a data source, click the orange tab with the Go to Worksheet annotation, at the bottom of the screen (labeled Sheet1 in Figure 3-8).

Figure 3-8. Go to Worksheet caption at the bottom of the Data Source interface

Clicking this tab takes you to the primary development interface, which is called the *Authoring interface*. If you ever need to return to the Data Source interface to make updates, such as removing or editing data source or extract filters, simply click the Data Source tab in the bottom-left corner of the screen.

CHAPTER 4

Tableau Terminology

The *Authoring interface*—named as such because you are *authoring* an analysis or story with your data—is the main place where you create visualizations in Tableau Desktop. In order to make progress, becoming acquainted with the various features of the Authoring interface is critical.

Data Pane

Under the top navigation menu and tool ribbon, you'll see the starting point for every view on the left side of the Authoring interface: the *Data pane* (Figure 4-1).

The first thing you'll see on the Data pane are all the data sources you have connected to. We have connected to only one data source so far, so we see Orders+ (the plus sign indicating we have connected to the Orders table and at least one additional table) from the Sample – Superstore Excel file. Farther down on the Data pane, you see all the fields available to analyze.

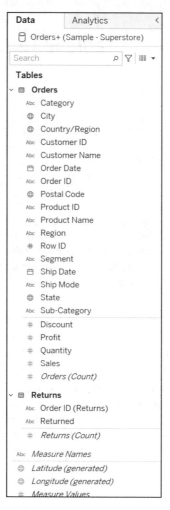

Figure 4-1. The Data pane in Tableau's Authoring interface

Fields

By default, the *fields* in our data source are organized into the respective tables they came from. If you prefer to organize your fields by folders, you can click the down arrow in the top-right corner of the Data pane and choose Group by Folder, as shown in Figure 4-2.

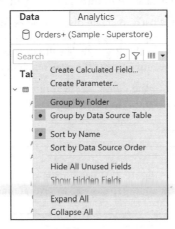

Figure 4-2. Grouping data fields by folder in Tableau Desktop

In addition to the fields you have grouped by either data source table or folder, you will see at least three generated fields in italics:

[Table Name] (Count):
　　A count of the rows in the table.

Measure Names:
　　Contains the names of the measures in the dataset. Chapter 5 describes measures in more detail.

Measure Values
　　Contains the values of the measures in the dataset.

These are called *generated* fields because Tableau automatically adds them to every dataset, regardless of its contents. If you are using any field with an assigned geographic role, such as Country, you will also see generated Latitude and Longitude fields.

Shelves

To use the fields in your dataset to create visualizations, you will drag and drop them to *shelves* and to the Marks card (detailed in the next section) throughout the interface.

The *Pages shelf* is used to create discrete views that can be flipped through to help understand patterns. For example, dragging Order Date to the Pages shelf will allow you to visualize one date at a time and animate the view much like a flipbook.

Any field added to the *Filters shelf* will filter the *marks*, or data points, being shown on the view. Chapter 10 describes filters in more detail.

Marks Card

The *Marks card* (Figure 4-3) has a drop-down list that allows you to change the mark type as well as several mark properties.

Figure 4-3. The Marks card with its mark type drop-down menu and default properties

---

This is called the Marks card because any changes you make here will influence how the *marks*—which, as I've said, you can think of as the data points on the view—are being encoded.

Changing the mark type from the default, Text, to something else, such as Bar, will change the Text property to Label. Dragging fields onto the Label property would then influence how the bars on the view are being labeled.

Changing the mark type to Line, Shape, Pie, or Polygon will result in a sixth Marks property of Path, Shape, Angle, or Path appearing, respectively.

Columns, Rows, and Chart Types

Perhaps the most useful features of the Authoring interface are the Columns and Rows shelves, shown in Figure 4-4, which lay the groundwork for every visualization you build in Tableau.

Figure 4-4. The Columns shelf and Rows shelf

Any field placed onto the Columns shelf will create a *column* on the view, and any field placed onto the Rows shelf will create a *row* on the view. These two shelves control the horizontal and vertical orientation of every chart.

NOTE

Fields placed onto the Pages, Filters, Columns, or Rows shelf or the Marks card inherit an oblong form. For this reason, the slang term *pill* is often used to describe fields being used in Tableau Desktop.

As an option to quickly create up to 24 popular chart types, you can click the Show Me button in the top-right corner of the Authoring interface, as shown in Figure 4-5.

Figure 4-5. Tableau's Show Me feature

Although this feature is helpful for efficiently starting various visualizations, Chapter 7 explains why you shouldn't rely exclusively on Show Me to author in Tableau. To help you understand how these various shelves and cards work together to create and encode visualizations, Chapter 7 through Chapter 9 will show you how to create some of the most effective visualizations manually.

CHAPTER 5

Dimension Versus Measure

Before we build our first chart type, you should know about the two major ways that Tableau classifies every field in a dataset. The first way is still the cornerstone of how I create every visualization in Tableau: dimension versus measure.

Using Measures

By default, Tableau classifies quantitative fields as measures. *Measures* are considered dependent because they tell us very little on their own. Consider the bar chart in Figure 5-1, showing the sum of the Profit measure across all the rows in the Sample – Superstore dataset.

You may feel very financially comfortable if this $286K value represents your annual salary, or a bit stressed out if this value represents your credit card debt—you just don't know!

Figure 5-1. Tableau bar chart showing the sum of the Profit measure

Without details about the measure value—including its name, the time range that the values span, the way the values are being aggregated (discussed in Chapter 7), which category we are analyzing, and so forth—this number is all but meaningless. Measures are dependent on the context that is provided by combining numerical values with dimensions.

Using Dimensions

By default, Tableau classifies qualitative fields and dates as dimensions. *Dimensions* are considered independent because some information about them is inherent. For example, the Category dimension in the Sample – Superstore dataset contains three dimension members: Furniture, Office Supplies, and Technology.

At some point in the business, somebody decided that certain products belong in these three categories, and that classification means something. However, measures and dimensions work best when used together. Consider Figure 5-2, which shows our sum of the Profit measure divided into the Furniture, Office Supplies, and Technology dimension members.

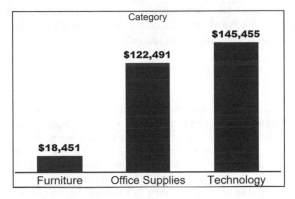

Figure 5-2. Bar chart showing the sum of the Profit measure divided by Category dimensions

Now that we are using at least one measure and one dimension together, we are able to glean insights about the business. In this case, Technology is the most profitable category, while Furniture is lagging way behind.

Making Classifications

As shown in Figure 5-3, dimensions and measures are separated by a horizontal rule on the Data pane.

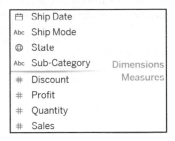

Figure 5-3. Dimensions and measures on the Data pane

Since, by default, quantitative fields are always classified as measures, and qualitative fields are always classified as dimensions, you occasionally must reclassify fields.

TIP

A quick rule of thumb to help you determine whether a measure should ever be reclassified as a dimension is to ask yourself, "Would it ever make sense to add these numbers up?" In the case of Customer Number, for example, it would not make sense to add Customer Number 1, to 2, to 3, to get to 6. Instead, I would start with a measure such as Profit, and break up that value by Customer Number to see how much profit I made per customer.

If you ever need to reclassify a field, right-click the field from within the Data pane and choose either Convert to Dimension or Convert to Measure (depending on which type of field you are converting). Alternatively, you can drag a field above or below the line on the Data pane that separates dimensions and measures to reclassify it.

The reason I consider this first classification the cornerstone for creating every visualization in Tableau is that I always add the *measures* that I want to analyze to the view first. I then add context to the analysis by breaking up those values by various *dimensions*.

Chapter 6 discusses the second major way that Tableau classifies every field being used and what generates the blue and green color-coding you see throughout Tableau.

Discrete Versus Continuous

The second major way Tableau classifies every field being used on a view is called *discrete versus continuous*. This classification is what the blue and green color-coding throughout Tableau Desktop's interfaces represent. Anytime you see blue, the field being used is discrete. Anytime you see green, the field being used is continuous.

Each classification has unique characteristics that will help you create every visualization in Tableau. Most notably, discrete fields draw headers that can be sorted, and continuous fields draw axes that cannot be sorted.

Visualizing Discrete and Continuous Options

Consider the bar chart in Figure 6-1, which shows the same example from Chapter 5, but here I have zoomed out to show you the y-axis, Columns shelf, and Rows shelf.

Note that the Category dimension is on the Columns shelf and colored blue. This means that Tableau is drawing a column for each category, and, because the field is discrete, Tableau is drawing discrete headers on those columns. If we wanted to, we could sort these discrete columns into ascending or descending order by their profit values.

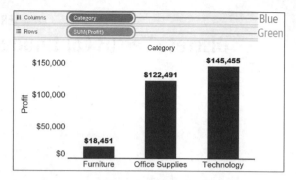

Figure 6-1. Bar chart in Tableau with discrete Category dimension on the Columns shelf and continuous Profit measure on the Rows shelf

The Profit measure, on the other hand, is on the Rows shelf and is colored green. This means that Tableau is drawing a row for the profit values, which creates a y-axis, and, because the field is continuous, Tableau is drawing a continuous axis that cannot be sorted. You cannot sort continuous fields because it would be extremely challenging to analyze this visualization if the values were not in continuous order (for example, $100,000, $0, $150,000, $50,000).

Changing Discrete and Continuous Options

Measures, bins (used to create histograms), and dates are unique in that they can be used as continuous or discrete fields. Consider Figure 6-2, where I have replaced the discrete Category field from Figure 6-1 with the continuous MONTH(Order Date) field.

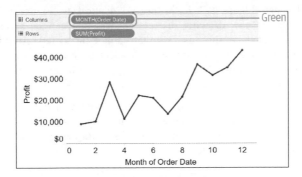

Figure 6-2. Line graph in Tableau showing profit by continuous date values

When dates are used as continuous fields, Tableau draws a continuous axis with the date's values (such as 1–12 for months). In this case, Tableau also automatically changed my mark type from Bar to Line, creating a line graph instead of bar chart.

If you were to change the MONTH(Order Date) field to discrete, which you can do by right clicking the field and choosing Discrete, Tableau draws discrete headers with the date's discrete parts, as Figure 6-3 shows.

Figure 6-3. Line graph in Tableau showing profit by discrete date parts

Although Figure 6-3 looks nearly identical to Figure 6-2, Tableau is now drawing discrete headers that can be sorted instead of a continuous axis that cannot be sorted. At this point, it is a coincidence that the headers are in chronological order, but technically there is no longer a continuous relationship from left to right.

In fact, if you were to sort these profit values in descending order as in Figure 6-4, Tableau automatically changes the mark type to Bar because the Line is mistakenly implying a relationship between the values.

Figure 6-4. Bar chart in Tableau showing profit by discrete month, sorted in descending order

To change the sort order of a discrete field, you can either click the ascending or descending icons on the tool ribbon at the top of the Authoring interface or right-click the field on the view and choose Sort. These options aren't available with continuous fields.

This chapter has used bar charts and line graphs to show you the consequences of using fields as discrete or continuous. The next two chapters go into greater detail, showing you several options for creating these essential visualizations.

CHAPTER 7

How to Make a Bar Chart

Bar charts, introduced in William Playfair's *The Commercial and Political Atlas* in 1786, have withstood the test of time for more than two centuries and are still an essential option for any visual analytics project today. In fact, the simple bar chart is the first chart type I try anytime I need to compare numerical values in categorical, or discrete, data. Bar charts are so effective because they leverage the preattentive attribute of height (when the chart is in a vertical orientation) or length (when the chart is in a horizontal orientation).

NOTE

Preattentive attributes are aspects of a visual that our visual processing system recognizes and is drawn to before slowing down for further, postattentive processing. Preattentive attributes such as height and length—not to mention others like color, size, and position—are processed extremely efficiently by the viewer, making them an ideal mechanism for communicating data.

Creating a Bar Chart

Bar charts are so pervasive and useful that they are the default chart type Tableau creates when you double-click a measure from within the Data pane, which is the first method for creating a bar chart in Tableau. In Figure 7-1, I have simply double-clicked the Profit measure from the Sample – Superstore dataset. The default behavior is for Tableau to place this measure on the Rows shelf with a mark type of Bar, creating a bar chart in a vertical orientation.

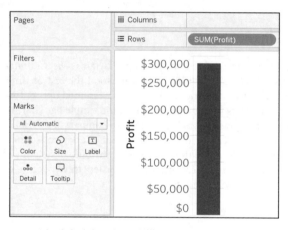

Figure 7-1. The default bar chart in Tableau, created by double-clicking the Profit measure from within the Data pane

You can create the exact same bar chart in at least two other ways. First, instead of double-clicking the field from the Data pane, you can left-click and drag the field to the Rows shelf or the "Drop field here" area on the y-axis. Alternatively, you can add the field to the view by double-clicking the Rows shelf, typing the exact name of the field, and pressing the Enter key twice. Tableau calls the latter approach adding a field *in the flow* of the analysis.

You can also change the orientation of this chart from vertical to horizontal in two ways. First, you can drag the pill that is on the Rows shelf to the Columns shelf, which will create an x-axis instead of a y-axis, changing the layout of the visualization. Alternatively, you can click the Swap Rows and Columns button, shown in Figure 7-2, which swaps everything on the Rows shelf with everything on the Columns shelf.

Figure 7-2. The Swap Rows and Columns button in Tableau

A common theme in Tableau is that there is always more than one way to do the same thing. We are already up to five ways to make a bar chart in Tableau, and we haven't even used the assistance of Show Me yet! With so many options, I always say the best way to do something in Tableau is the way you are comfortable with that provides the correct answer.

Introducing Aggregation in Tableau

If you look closely at the Profit pill on the view, you'll see that the name of the field is preceded by the aggregation SUM. By default, every measure in Tableau is aggregated, and the default aggregation is SUM, which adds up all the values. I think of *aggregation* as consolidating several rows into one. For example, if we have three rows of profit values—$50, $100, and $150 summing the values on those three rows would create a single value of $300.

If you prefer to not aggregate the values, so as to visualize each unique value, click Analysis in the top navigation menu and then deselect Aggregate Measures. If you choose not to aggregate values, Tableau will automatically change the mark type to Shape to help you visualize one mark per value rather than a single aggregated bar.

TIP

You can change a measure's default aggregation by right-clicking it from within the Data pane and then selecting Default Properties > Aggregation to access and choose an alternative.

There are also two ways to choose an aggregation other than the default. First, if you've already added a measure to the view, you can either right-click its pill or click the down arrow that appears when hovering over the pill. As shown in Figure 7-3, this reveals several options for the field, including its aggregation, which you can change by hovering over the current aggregation and then choosing an alternative.

Alternatively, if you were building the bar chart from scratch again, you could *right-click* a measure while dragging it onto the Rows shelf or Columns shelf. Tableau will give you the options for aggregating the measure before anything is drawn on the view—a sixth way to make a bar chart!

Figure 7-3. Changing the aggregation of a field already on the view

Combining Measures and Dimensions to Glean Insight

Now that we have a *measure* on the view, we can add context and glean insight by adding a *dimension* to either the Rows shelf or Columns shelf. In Figure 7-4, I have added the Category dimension to the Columns shelf. This divides the sum of profit values into one column per discrete category. Because the mark type is still Bar, we can compare the heights of each bar to analyze the business, just as we did in Chapter 5.

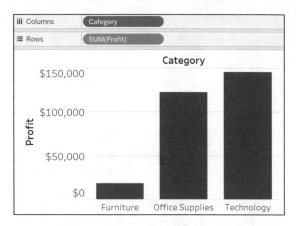

Figure 7-4. Bar chart showing the sum of profit values by category

This chapter has shown you six ways to make a bar chart and introduced how aggregation works in Tableau. The bar chart is one of the most effective choices for categorical analyses. In Chapter 8, you will learn one of the essential visualizations for time-series analyses: the line graph.

How to Make a Line Graph

Like the bar chart, the line graph was one of the original data visualizations introduced in William Playfair's *The Commercial and Political Atlas* in 1786 and has remained a staple for data visualization practitioners to this day. The *line graph* plots points at the intersection of values on a vertical y-axis and horizontal x-axis and then connects those points with straight lines. Viewing the vertical location of values on the y-axis and how those values are changing from left to right on the x-axis makes the line graph ideal for analyzing trends over time.

As with the bar chart in Chapter 7, you can go about making a line graph in several ways in Tableau. To start, in Figure 8-1 I've double-clicked the Profit measure on the Data pane from the Sample – Superstore dataset. This action has placed the Profit measure on the Rows shelf with an aggregation of SUM, and the visualization has a mark type of Bar.

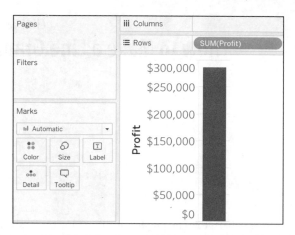

Figure 8-1. The default bar chart in Tableau, created by double-clicking the Profit measure from within the Data pane

My preferred method for creating a line graph is to right-click and drag my date dimension from the Data pane to the Columns shelf. I prefer this method because Tableau gives you the option to choose whether to use discrete date parts or continuous date values, as well as the granularity of the date (such as day, week, month, and so on), before it draws anything.

Figure 8-2 shows the options that appear after holding the right mouse button while dragging the Order Date dimension in the sample data from the Data pane to the Columns shelf.

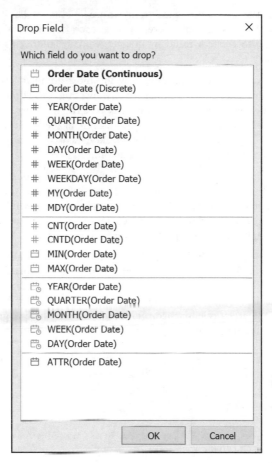

Figure 8-2. Options for discrete date parts and continuous date values for a Tableau line graph

This list may look intimidating at first, but we can quickly narrow these options to our preferred selection. Let's assume we want to make a line graph that looks at a continuous profit trend by quarter. The first option, Order Date (Continuous), will create the chronological trend we are looking for, but it will show the most granular level of data: each day. Since we are looking to create a trend by quarter, we can ignore this first option.

The second option will also show the most granular level of data, and it has a blue icon next to it, indicating it will draw discrete headers instead of a continuous axis. In fact, every option with a blue icon next to it will draw discrete headers that can be sorted. If you want to draw a continuous axis that cannot be sorted, you can ignore 10 of these 20 options.

The third section in the dialog contains aggregations you would use on a measure, such as count, count distinct, minimum, and maximum. Although those can also be useful with dates, they are irrelevant for our current use case of creating a line graph that looks at profit by continuous quarter.

That leaves us with the fourth section, then. Each of these five choices will draw a continuous axis in chronological order that cannot be sorted, and all we have to do is choose the appropriate level of granularity. After clicking the QUARTER option with the green calendar icon, Figure 8-3 shows the line graph that Tableau will create.

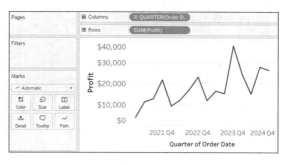

Figure 8-3. Line graph depicting the sum of profit values by continuous quarter

It's that easy to create one of the most effective options for analyzing trends over time, but let me show you some additional ways to create line graphs.

Tableau Line Graph Defaults

To lay the foundation of the first example, I double-clicked the Profit measure, which added it to the Rows shelf and created the y-axis. If I were to also double-click the date dimension instead of holding the right mouse key while dragging it onto the Columns shelf, we would get a different view. Figure 8-4 shows the default settings of a line graph created by double-clicking a date dimension.

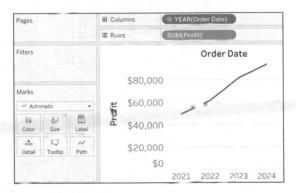

Figure 8-4. Line graph showing the sum of profit values by discrete year

While we have an x-axis and a mark type of Line, these defaults differ from our first version of the line graph in two respects. First, the default date part is year instead of quarter. Second, the pill is blue instead of green, indicating we are drawing discrete headers that can be sorted instead of a continuous axis that cannot be sorted.

To either change the granularity of the date dimension or flip it from discrete to continuous, you can either right-click the dimension's pill or click the down arrow that appears when hovering over the pill. Figure 8-5 shows the options after taking either of these two actions.

Figure 8-5. Discrete date part and continuous date value options

The first set of date options will draw discrete date parts. As you can see, we have selected discrete Year, which is why the date dimension is colored blue and drawing discrete headers. The second set of date options will draw continuous date values. If I were to click the second occurrence of Quarter, the line graph would return to the exact same line graph created with my preferred method discussed earlier.

Using the Show Me Feature

To this point, I have purposely built my two favorite chart types manually to help illustrate how Tableau works, but you can also automatically generate 24 popular chart types by using *Show Me* (introduced in Chapter 4). Located in the top-right corner of the Authoring interface, you can use Show Me to either change visualizations already on the view or start a visualization from scratch.

To illustrate the latter, I have preselected the two fields used in the first two examples by clicking the Order Date dimension on the Data pane, and then holding the Ctrl key while clicking the Profit measure. With these two fields selected, Figure 8-6 shows the Show Me options, which you can view by clicking the Show Me button in the top-right corner of the Authoring interface.

The thumbnail images in color are the visualizations you can draw with the preselected fields (or fields being used on the view if you've already created a visualization). If a thumbnail is grayed out, you do not have the correct combination of dimensions and/or measures to create that visualization. You can see the combination of fields required to draw a visualization by hovering over any of the thumbnails.

Figure 8-6. Tableau's Show Me options

Tableau also draws an orange border around its recommended visualization. With Order Date and Profit selected, Tableau is recommending the default, discrete line graph, which we built in the second example. If you preferred to draw a continuous date axis like the first example in this chapter, you would need to click the Lines (Continuous) thumbnail, the option just to the left of the recommendation. Figure 8-7 shows the line graph Show Me generates after choosing Lines (Continuous) with the Order Date and Profit fields preselected.

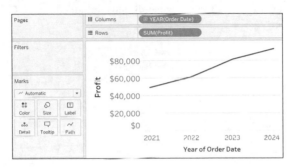

Figure 8-7. Line graph depicting the sum of profit values by continuous year

If we want to match the original use case in this chapter, sum of profit by continuous quarter, Show Me has us close, but we still need to click into the date pill and change the granularity of the date to quarter. Show Me is a great option for efficiently starting 24 popular chart types, but you do need to know how Tableau ticks to get the exact results you're looking for.

TIP

While I don't recommend using Show Me exclusively, it is very helpful in teaching you the types of fields needed to create various charts and showing where Tableau will place pills to generate them on the view. I also suggest using Show Me to create simple crosstabs, or text tables, to verify numbers as you author in Tableau, which you can do by clicking the very first Show Me option.

Adding Context to a Line Graph by Encoding Marks

With any of these three options for making a line graph in Tableau, you can easily create comparisons by dragging a dimension to the Color property on the Marks card. Figure 8-8 shows a line graph illustrating the sum of the profit by continuous quarter, with the Category dimension added to the Color property.

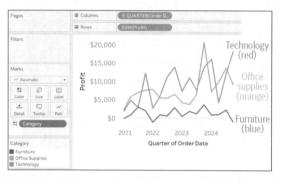

Figure 8-8. Tableau line graph depicting the sum of the profit by continuous quarter, colored by category

With the line graph plotting profit values by continuous quarter, and now colored by our three Category dimension members, we can see that Furniture has consistently trailed the other categories and even had unprofitable quarters. (This book is printed in black-and-white, but each of the three lines is a different color onscreen.)

Formatting Tips for Line Graphs

I'll close this chapter by sharing formatting ideas for line graphs, some of which can be applied to other visualizations. First, you can remap the default colors assigned to dimension members by clicking the Color property on the Marks card or double-clicking any of the squares in the color legend that appear after adding a field to the Color property. With the Edit Colors dialog open, select a dimension member first and then assign a color to it on the right. You can also use custom colors by double-clicking the dimension member and assigning an HSV (hue, saturation, values), RGB (red, green, blue), or hex code value.

I also recommend experimenting with the line weights by clicking the Size property on the Marks card and moving the slider that appears from left to right. Dragging the slider to the right will make the mark weight heavier, making the lines appear wider; dragging the slider to the left will make the mark weight lighter, making the lines appear thinner.

Lastly, you can access an effect called *Markers* by clicking the Color property on the Marks card. Choosing the second of three marker options will add a small circle to each intersection plotted on the axes. These markers serve the practical purpose of showing you the locations of data points—plus they give line graphs some professional polish! Figure 8-9 shows just how far these quick formatting tips can take a visualization.

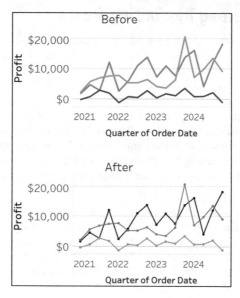

Figure 8-9. Tableau line graph before and after applying formatting tips

CHAPTER 9

How to Make a Scatter Plot

A *scatter plot* visualizes the intersection of points across two variables, each represented by its own continuous axis. This chart type has at least four major benefits:

- Demonstrates correlations between the two variables
- Creates a four-quadrant segmentation
- Indicates outliers
- Visualizes many data points in a small space

This chapter shows how to make a scatter plot, discusses how aggregations are affected by the visualization's level of detail, and introduces the Analytics pane.

To start a scatter plot, place a measure on the Rows shelf and a second measure on the Columns shelf. Figure 9-1 shows a default scatter plot in Tableau after placing the Profit measure on the Rows shelf with an aggregation of Average, and the Discount measure on the Columns shelf with an aggregation of Average.

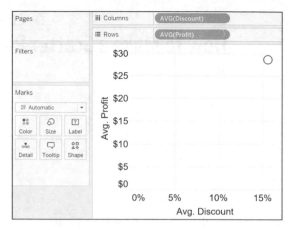

Figure 9-1. The default scatter plot in Tableau with AVG(Profit) on the Rows shelf and AVG(Discount) on the Columns shelf

---

TIP

It is considered best practice to place your *dependent measure* on the Rows shelf, which forms the y-axis, and the *explanatory measure* on the Columns shelf, which forms the x-axis. In this case, we are evaluating profit and seeing whether a correlation exists with the Discount measure that helps explain the profit values.

Another best practice with scatter plots is to make them square (with the height of the y-axis equal to the width of the x-axis), so as to not skew a potential correlation.

Visualization Level of Detail

Every visualization you create in Tableau has what's called a *level of detail*. I think of level of detail as synonymous with the most granular level of the analysis at hand. This is a critical concept to grasp because, by default, every aggregation in Tableau is done at the visualization level of detail.

In the case of our scatter plot, we have not yet specified any thing more granular than the entire dataset. This means when we see the Profit measure on the Rows shelf with an aggregation of Average, the value on the y-axis represents the average profit values across all 9,994 records in the Sample – Superstore dataset being used. The value on the x-axis represents the average discount values across every record; then Tableau has plotted a single mark at the intersection of the *x* and *y* values.

Anytime you add a dimension to the Rows shelf, Columns shelf, or Marks card, you make the visualization's level of detail more granular, and thus change the level of aggregation. Figure 9-2 shows how the scatter plot looks after placing the State dimension onto the Detail property of the Marks card, increasing the visualization's level of detail (the granularity of the analysis).

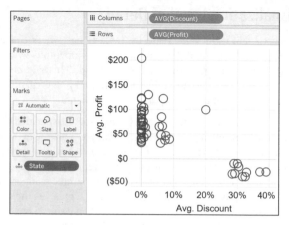

Figure 9-2. AVG(Profit) and AVG(Discount) scatter plot aggregated at the State level of detail

Now instead of visualizing the averages across the entire dataset, Tableau is visualizing the averages at the state level and plotting a mark for each state. In this scenario, the scatter plot has helped us identify a potential correlation. It seems the higher the average discount, the lower the average profit value. Let's make this analysis more scientific by using the Analytics pane to test our hypothesis.

Getting Started with the Analytics Pane

To this point in the book, we have relied exclusively on the Data pane for our analyses. Though this is the primary area to begin visualizations and leverage the technical features found in later chapters, the *Analytics pane* is also helpful in bringing your analyses to life.

The Analytics pane contains several drag-and-drop summary and modeling features that you can access by clicking the Analytics tab, which is to the right of the Data tab, in the top-left corner of the Authoring interface. Figure 9-3 shows the features available on the Analytics pane.

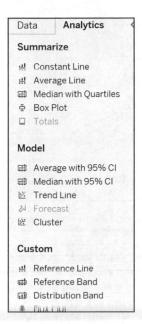

Figure 9-3. Summarize, Model, and Custom features on the Analytics pane

To use any of these features, left-click and drag them onto a visualization. Like the Show Me options described in Chapter 8, grayed-out features indicate those options are not relevant with the combination of fields being used on the view. Figure 9-4 shows how my scatter plot looks after dragging the Trend Line feature onto the view and choosing a Linear trend line. Hovering the mouse pointer over the trend line reveals details about its model in the tooltip.

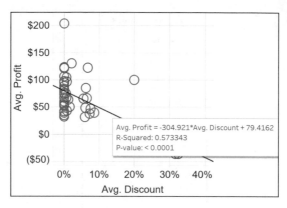

Figure 9-4. Adding a trend line from the Analytics pane and hovering over the line to view the tooltip

The extremely low p-value indicates there is a very low chance that average profit and average discount are not correlated. Visualizing correlations is one major benefit of using scatter plots, and we have made the analysis even better by supporting it with statistics available from the Analytics pane.

NOTE

A p-value of < 0.05 is a widely used benchmark for determining correlation, but lower values like 0.01 can be used if you want to be more confident in your conclusion, and higher values like 0.10 can be used if you do not need to be as precise.

Another useful option on the Analytics pane is Average Line, which draws a reference line across the view at the average value of the axis it is added to. In Figure 9-5, I have left-clicked and dragged Average Line from the Analytics pane onto the scatter plot.

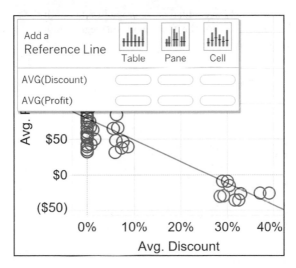

Figure 9-5. Adding an Average line from the Analytics pane to an axis

The interface that appears can look intimidating because of its six options for where to draw the reference line, but you are simply choosing the axis to add it to and the scope of the analysis.

Various scopes are created when you add fields to either the Rows or Columns shelf. In our scenario, we have not broken up the Profit axis by additional fields to create separate panes or cells, so any of the three options for that axis will draw the same line.

If this is confusing to you, you can add the same type of line by right-clicking directly on the axis you want to add the line to and choosing Add Reference Line. You can also edit these lines after they are on a view by right-clicking them directly and choosing Edit or by right-clicking the axis containing the reference line and choosing Edit Reference Line.

In Figure 9-6, I have added an Average line for both the x-axis and y-axis to create the four-quadrant segmentation I mentioned in this chapter's introduction.

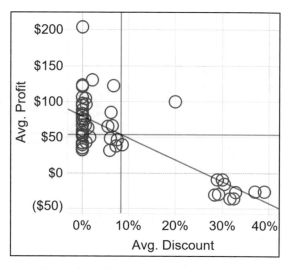

Figure 9-6. Scatter plot with Average lines on the x-axis and y-axis

These reference lines have created four segments:

- High average profit and low average discount in the top-left quadrant
- High average profit and high average discount in the top-right quadrant
- Low average profit and high average discount in the bottom-right quadrant
- Low average profit and low average discount in the bottom-left quadrant

Segments like these are very actionable because we may want to treat the dimension members in these four quadrants differently from each other. For example, the mark in the top-right quadrant (the state of Wyoming) seems to be less sensitive to discounting; perhaps we can reduce the average discount and make even more profit.

NOTE

Further, the segment in the bottom-right quadrant is costing the company profit, and the trend line has helped us understand that's likely due to the high average discount. The first thing I would do at this company is experiment with the average discount in those states to see if we can turn them profitable!

Closing Thoughts on Chart Types

The charts covered to this point can be formatted in infinite ways, and many more visualizations can be created in Tableau. In fact, my first two books, *Practical Tableau* and *Innovative Tableau* (both published by O'Reilly), contain 29 and 36 tutorials, respectively, on chart types alone.

That being said, I believe visualizations are yet another thing in business that follows the 80/20 rule. Equipped with the bar chart, line graph, and scatter plot, I believe you can answer roughly 80% of business questions that emerge! For this reason, I have shared my three favorite chart types in this pocket reference. The rest of this book focuses on the essential technical features that will help you get the most out of any visualization.

CHAPTER 10

Filters

Tableau is built on a patented technology called *VizQL*, which translates what a user is dragging and dropping onto the view into database queries like those in Structured Query Language (SQL). The result of those queries is then reflected on the view as a data visualization. Instead of using a series of WHERE clauses as you would in SQL, a Tableau user can filter out marks on a view by dragging and dropping a field onto the Filters shelf and setting their criteria in user-friendly dialogs. This chapter explains the four core types of Tableau filters, options for scaling filters across a workbook, and how to understand Tableau's filter order of operations.

Types of Filters

Tableau allows a user to filter marks on a view based on measure values or dimension members. You can also filter rows from the dataset before arriving in the Authoring interface with a data source or extract filter. In Chapter 9, we discovered a correlation between average profit and average discount. If we want to focus on only the states with a profit of less than zero, we can drag the Profit measure from the Data pane to the Filters shelf, which will create our first measure filter.

Upon adding a measure to the Filters shelf, Tableau will ask you to choose the aggregation of the measure. As with the fields we've added to the Rows shelf and Columns shelf, this aggregation is done at the visualization level of detail. In the case of our scatter plot, the most granular level of the analysis is the State dimension, meaning the aggregation we choose now and the values we set in the next dialog will be considered for each *state*. Figure 10-1 shows the options for a measure filter after choosing an aggregation of Average.

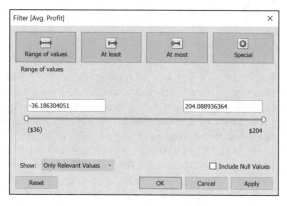

Figure 10-1. Measure filter options for average profit

By default, we are seeing the full range of profit values at the state level, which can be filtered by moving the sliders and/or typing different values for the start and end of the range. You can also use the "At least" button to set only the start of the range, the "At most" button to set only the end of the range, or the Special button to filter null or non-null values. Figure 10-2 shows the scatter plot from Chapter 9 after adding a measure filter for average profit and setting the end of the range to zero.

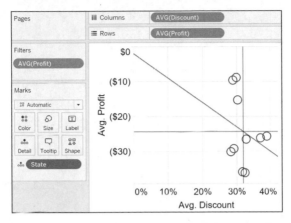

Figure 10-2. Average Profit by Average Discount scatter plot, filtered to average profit less than zero

With this measure filter in place, we can focus on the worst-performing states to see if we can improve profitability.

Dimension filters can also be added by dragging a dimension from the Data pane to the Filters shelf. For this example, I have returned to the line graph created in Chapter 8. Let's assume we are the managers of the Technology category and want to filter the line graph to display only the trend for what's under our control. Figure 10-3 shows the dimension filter options that appear after dragging the Category dimension from the Data pane to the Filters shelf.

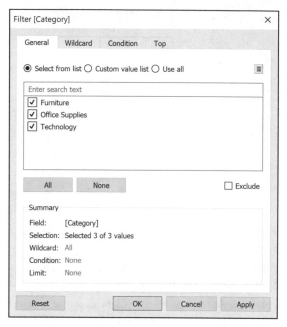

Figure 10-3. Dimension filter options for the Category field

Dimension filters contain four tabs of options:

General

Allows you to pick and choose individual dimension members to include or exclude

Wildcard

Allows you to use string functions to keep or exclude dimension members that contain, start with, end with, or exactly match specific letters

Condition

Allows you to specify numerical thresholds or conditional logic for keeping dimension members

Top

> Allows you to keep a top or bottom *N* (number) for a specific field

To demonstrate the functionality of the General tab, I have deselected the Furniture and Office Supplies categories, leaving Figure 10-4 with only the Technology category.

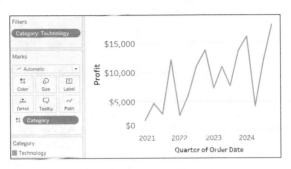

Figure 10-4. Line graph with a dimension filter

With the trend filtered to only the Technology category, as the managers of the category, we can analyze only what is relevant to us.

Options for Scaling Filters

By default, filters apply to only the sheet where they are originally added, but you have the option to carry over the same logic to two or more worksheets in the workbook. To access these options, click into a filter on the Filters shelf (either by right-clicking or hovering the mouse pointer over a filter and clicking the down arrow that appears) and select Apply to Worksheets. In Figure 10-5, I have clicked into the dimension filter on our line graph to see the options I have for applying the same filter to other worksheets in the workbook.

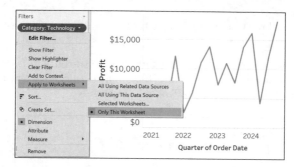

Figure 10-5. Options for applying filters to other worksheets

As pictured, the default behavior is for Tableau to apply the filter to only the sheet it has been added to. The remaining options go in order from the lowest to highest scaling:

Selected Worksheets
    Allows you to pick and choose specific sheets to apply the filter.

All Using This Data Source
    Applies the filter logic to any worksheet in the workbook that was built with the data source containing the field

All Using Related Data Sources
    Applies the filter criteria to any sheet in the workbook that has the same field, even if the field is in multiple data sources

As manager of the Technology category, I may choose to apply this dimension filter to all sheets using this data source. Since we are using a single data source, this option would make the Category filter global and filter our bar chart, line graph, and scatter plot to only the Technology category.

Understanding Tableau's Filter Order of Operations

You can add as many filters as you want to the Filters shelf, but it can be challenging to track which filters are doing what and in what order. The key to understanding which filters are actually filtering marks on the view is Tableau's *order of operations*. Figure 10-6 shows Tableau's order of operations with the different types of filters highlighted. The higher in this order of operations, the earlier the filter is applied.

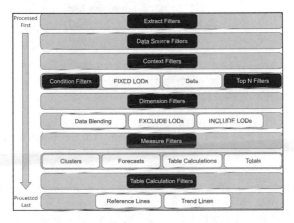

Figure 10-6. Tableau's order of operations with types of filters highlighted

To demonstrate how these filters work together within Tableau's order of operations, I have created the bar chart in Figure 10-7. Here, the Sales measure is shown with the Product Name and Category dimensions, sorted in descending order.

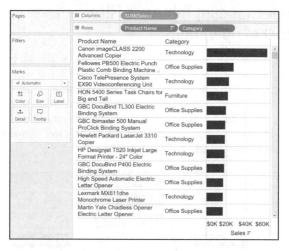

Figure 10-7. Tableau bar chart with no filters applied

With the combination of Product Name and Category on the Rows shelf, we see 1,849 rows of marks. This results in a long, vertical scroll bar on the right and an unpleasant user experience.

To limit the number of rows, I drag the Sales measure from the Data pane to the Filters shelf, choose an aggregation of Sum, and set the minimum value to 5,000. Figure 10-8 shows the settings of this measure filter.

After clicking the OK button to apply the filter, I am left with 107 rows. This is a substantial improvement, because the 107 rows will be much easier to compare than all 1,849. But let's limit the rows even more by focusing on the top 10 products.

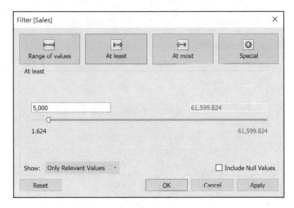

Figure 10-8. Measure filter keeping marks with values of at least 5,000

To do so, I drag the Product Name dimension from the Data pane to the Filters shelf, navigate to the Top tab, and set up the criteria to keep only the top 10 by Sum of Sales. Figure 10-9 shows the settings of this Top *N* filter.

We now have two filters on the Filters shelf, but because of Tableau's order of operations, the Top *N* filter is limiting the view to the top 10 product names *before* the measure filter limits the marks to those above $5,000 in sales. Since the lowest value in the top 10 is $17,000 (i.e., already above $5,000), the measure filter is not doing anything in this scenario.

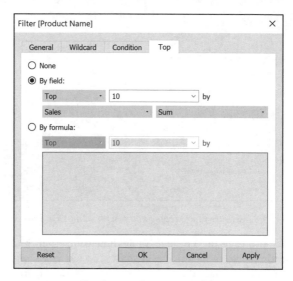

Figure 10-9. Top N filter keeping the top 10 product names by sum of sales

---

NOTE

Considering how each filter fits into the order of operations helps determine which filters should be kept on the Filters shelf. In this scenario, we can remove the measure filter, and the view will not change at all. If the top 10 will eventually be filtered to values less than $5,000 and/or we decide to move the minimum value of the measure filter above 17,000, we should keep the measure filter.

As an analyst, the next logical question I have is, "What is the top 10 for a specific category?" Let's again assume we're the managers of the Technology category, so we drag the Category dimension from the Data pane to the Filters shelf and keep only the Technology dimension member selected on the

General tab. Figure 10-10 shows the bar chart with the combination of filters added during this chapter.

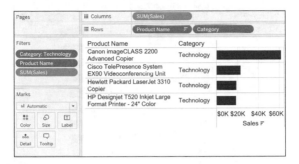

Figure 10-10. Bar chart filtered to the top 10 product names and Technology category

You were likely expecting to see 10 bars, but we see only four. What's happening is our Top *N* filter, Product Name, is filtering the product names to those in the top 10 before our dimension filter, Category, filters to the Technology category. What we are left with are the four Technology product names that are also in the top 10.

To get the expected result and see only the top 10 for a specific category, we must elevate the Category dimension filter in the order of operations. To do so, we will convert this dimension filter to a context filter, which you can do by right-clicking any dimension filter on the Filters shelf and choosing Add to Context.

Context filters get a special gray color-coding and are the first type of filter to execute on the Filters shelf. Figure 10-11 shows our top 10 products in the Technology category after changing the Category dimension filter to a context filter.

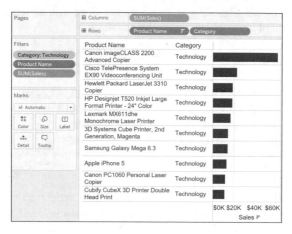

Figure 10-11. Bar chart filtered to the top 10 product names and Technology category, with the Category filter added to context

The context filter not only helped us get our expected result, but also can have real efficiency benefits when used to reduce the size of a dataset by at least 10%. When a filter is added to context, Tableau limits the number of rows that every subsequent filter queries. In this scenario, the Product Name and Sales filters are happening on the remaining 1,847 rows containing the Technology dimension member instead of the original 9,994 rows in the entire dataset.

Before you get the great idea to just add every filter to context, remember that elevating a second dimension filter to a context filter will have them competing in the order of operations again!

Any of the filters covered to this point can be shown to yourself and your workbook users by right-clicking them from within the Filters shelf and choosing Show Filter. This provides one-click access to defining the criteria that will keep or exclude marks from the view.

Data Source and Extract Filters

The last two types of filters, data source and extract, happen on the Data Source interface, which you can return to at any time by clicking the Data Source tab in the bottom-left corner of the Authoring interface. Figure 10-12 shows the two types of data connections and where to add a data source filter from the top-right corner of the Data Source interface.

Connection			Filters	
⦿ Live	○ Extract		0	Add

Figure 10-12. Types of data connections and where to add a data source filter

As discussed in Chapter 3, if you click the Add button, you are creating a data source filter. With the Extract radio button selected, you will see an Edit button appear where you can add an extract filter. Both of these happen first in the order of operations because they are filtering out rows of data before you begin analyzing further in the Authoring interface.

With these filter options in mind and an understanding of how they fit together in Tableau's order of operations, you will be able to focus on what's relevant to you, quickly pivot through analyses, and have your views processing as efficiently as possible.

CHAPTER 11

Calculated Fields

Calculated fields are custom fields created by a Tableau author. This feature has infinite applications, including the capabilities to do all of the following:

- Aggregate data in custom ways
- Clean up underlying data (such as inconsistent spellings)
- Use logic to create custom outcomes
- Segment underlying data without restructuring it outside Tableau
- Make Tableau do your math (for example, compute ratios)

There are three core types of calculated fields, each with its own unique uses and benefits:

- Basic calculations
- Table calculations
- Level of Detail calculations

This chapter provides an introduction and discusses applications of each type of calculated field.

Basic Calculated Fields

Basic calculated fields, the most common calculated field, fall into two categories: aggregate calculated fields and row-level calculated fields. The former aggregates multiple rows into single values, and the latter creates an outcome at an individual row-level.

Aggregate Calculated Fields

For the first example, let's say we want to create a measure that counts the number of orders in the Sample – Superstore dataset. By default, there are no measures called *orders*, but we can create a calculated field that counts the distinct dimension members in the Order ID dimension. You can start a calculated field in multiple ways, including the following:

- Right-click in any blank space on the Data pane and choose Create Calculated Field.
- Click the down arrow in the top-right corner of the Data pane and choose Create Calculated Field.
- Click Analysis from the top navigation menu and choose Create Calculated Field.

As a shortcut, if you know one of the existing fields that you are going to use in a calculated field, you can right-click that field directly within the Data pane and choose Create > Create Calculated Field. This saves you a few keystrokes because the field is automatically added to the calculated field dialog. Figure 11-1 shows the calculated field dialog after using this shortcut with the Order ID field and naming the new calculation `Unique Orders`.

Figure 11-1. Calculated field dialog

The formula to compute unique orders is COUNTD([Order ID]). This will aggregate the Order ID dimension members at the visualization level of detail with an aggregation of COUNTD, or *Count Distinct*.

Aggregations and functions are colored blue within calculated fields, and existing fields are colored orange. If you ever see an aggregation or function you are not familiar with, you can click it, and Tableau will look it up for you in the flyout on the right. This provides a brief description and how to use the function or aggregation within the syntax. Figure 11-2 shows my aggregate calculated field with COUNTD looked up in the data dictionary on the right.

Figure 11-2. Calculated field dialog with COUNTD definition and syntax

This Calculation Contains Errors

If you see a red error message in the lower-left corner of the calculated field dialog reading "The calculation contains errors,"
you can click the message to see what may be wrong with the
formula.

When you see the text "The calculation is valid" in the lower-
left corner of the interface, you have met the technical criteria
for Tableau to do the calculation, but this does not always mean
that the outcome is what you are expecting! It is always a good
idea to quality-check your calculations by using them on views
and checking the outcomes yourself.

After clicking the OK button in the calculated field dialog, I
find a new field on the Data pane called Unique Orders.
Because the result of my calculation is quantitative, it has been
classified as a measure and has a green number sign (#) before
its name.

When viewed on the Data pane, calculated fields are preceded
with an equal sign (=) and can be edited at any time by right-
clicking them and choosing Edit. Once you are ready to use a
calculated field, you can use them just like any other field by
adding them to the view or within other calculated fields.
Figure 11-3 shows a bar chart using this newly created calculated field aggregated at the Segment level.

The *AGG* preceding the name of the field on the Columns shelf
is telling us the field is being aggregated within the calculated
field. With Tableau now counting the number of distinct order
IDs at the Segment level, we have visibility to see that the Con-
sumer segment is leading the way, followed by Corporate and
Home Office.

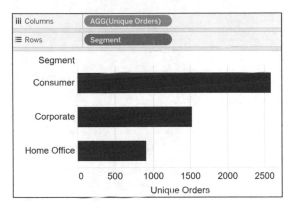

Figure 11-3. Unique Orders by Segment bar chart

TIP

What's best about calculated fields is you have to create them only once, and you can use them over and over again across views!

Row-Level Calculated Fields

The second type of calculated field computes an outcome for every row in the data. These are a good option if you want to segment or reclassify your dimensions without having to re-create the underlying data, but can also be used with measures. Figure 11-4 shows an example of a row-level calculation; I have classified every customer name that starts with an A as an **A Customer**, every customer name that starts with a B or a C as **B+C Customers**, and every other customer name as **Other**.

Customer Name Aliases
IF STARTSWITH([Customer Name],'a') THEN "A Customer"
ELSEIF STARTSWITH([Customer Name],'b') OR STARTSWITH([Customer Name],'c') THEN "B+C Customers"
ELSE "Other"
END
The calculation is valid.
Apply
OK

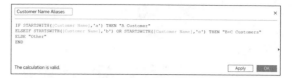

Figure 11-4. Row-level calculated field

TIP

Calculated fields have infinite applications that can be created from all the functions and aggregations found in the data dictionary on the right side of the calculated field dialog. I recommend taking time to explore the functions available in this interface.

As I do with aggregate calculated fields, I like to quality-check row-level calculated fields, which I do by placing the original field on the Rows shelf first followed by the newly created row-level calculated field second. Figure 11-5 shows that the custom aliases created in the calculated field are working as expected.

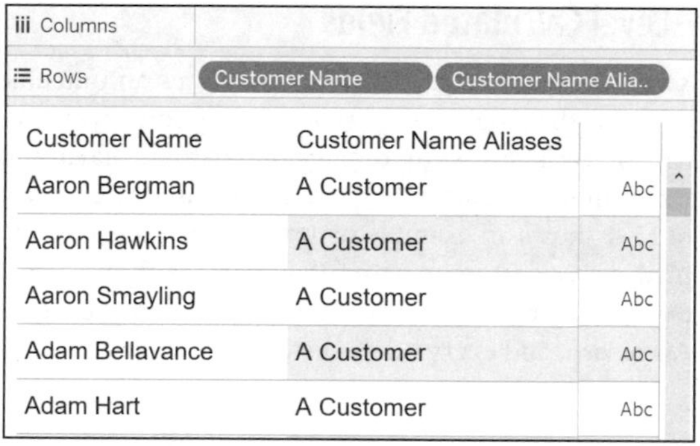

Columns
Rows
Customer Name
Customer Name Alia..
Customer Name
Customer Name Aliases
Aaron Bergman
A Customer
Abc
Aaron Hawkins
A Customer
Abc
Aaron Smayling
A Customer
Abc
Adam Bellavance
A Customer
Abc
Adam Hart
A Customer
Abc

Figure 11-5. Quality-checking a row-level calculated field

Because row-level calculated fields have an outcome for every row in the data, we can also check that the calculated field is working by viewing the dataset itself. To do so, you can either right-click the data source on the Data pane and choose View Data or click the table icon () in the top-right corner of the Data pane. Figure 11-6 shows the underlying data with an outcome of the Customer Name Aliases calculation on every row.

Category	City	Country/Region	Customer ID	Customer Name	Customer Name Aliases
Furniture	Henderson	United States	CG-12520	Claire Gute	B+C Customers
Furniture	Henderson	United States	CG-12520	Claire Gute	B+C Customers
Office Supplies	Los Angeles	United States	DV-13045	Darrin Van Huff	Other
Furniture	Fort Lauderdale	United States	SO-20335	Sean O'Donnell	Other
Office Supplies	Fort Lauderdale	United States	SO-20335	Sean O'Donnell	Other
Furniture	Los Angeles	United States	BH-11710	Brosina Hoffman	B+C Customers
Office Supplies	Los Angeles	United States	BH-11710	Brosina Hoffman	B+C Customers
Technology	Los Angeles	United States	BH-11710	Brosina Hoffman	B+C Customers
Office Supplies	Los Angeles	United States	BH-11710	Brosina Hoffman	B+C Customers
Office Supplies	Los Angeles	United States	BH-11710	Brosina Hoffman	B+C Customers
Furniture	Los Angeles	United States	BH-11710	Brosina Hoffman	B+C Customers
Technology	Los Angeles	United States	BH-11710	Brosina Hoffman	B+C Customers
Office Supplies	Concord	United States	AA-10480	Andrew Allen	A Customer
Office Supplies	Seattle	United States	IM-15070	Irene Maddox	Other
Office Supplies	Fort Worth	United States	HP-14815	Harold Pawlan	Other
Office Supplies	Fort Worth	United States	HP-14815	Harold Pawlan	Other

Figure 11-6. Viewing the Sample – Superstore data with a row-level calculated field

With the confidence that this new calculated field is working, we can use this custom segmentation just as we would use any dimension. Further, we can combine both types of basic calculated fields to see how many unique orders we had for our A Customer, B+C Customers, and Other segments—a completely custom analysis we can now do without any restructuring of the data!

Table Calculations

Table calculations are computed only on the table of data generating the view. One big benefit is that they process very efficiently because Tableau has to do the math on only a small subset of the data. This type of calculation also allows you to use and learn relatively advanced formulas even if you are just getting started with Tableau's syntax.

For this example, I set up a table in Figure 11-7 showing the Unique Orders calculated field from earlier in this chapter, broken down by the Segment and Year of Order Date dimensions.

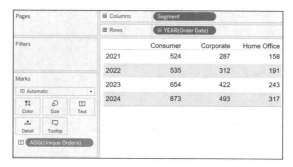

Figure 11-7. Text table showing Unique Orders by Segment and Year of Order Date

Table calculations are not limited to literal text table views in Tableau, but crosstabs like this do make it easier to demonstrate how they work and to ensure they are computing the expected results. Table calculations are added to measures by right-clicking their pills and choosing either Add Table Calculation or hovering over Quick Table Calculation and choosing one of the 11 commonly used table calculations.

For this use case, I'll say I want to calculate the running total of unique orders for each segment from 2021 to 2024. Figure 11-8 shows the result after right-clicking the Unique Orders pill that is currently on the Marks card's Text property and selecting Quick Table Calculation > Running Total.

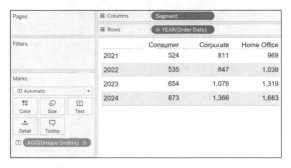

Figure 11-8. Text table showing running total of Unique Orders by Segment and Year of Order Date

The delta symbol (Δ) on the Unique Orders pill indicates that a table calculation is being computed. I also see that the numbers have changed, but it appears the running totals are being computed across the view from left to right, which is not the running total by year I was going for.

Table calculations are defined by how they are *addressed* (computed) and *partitioned* (grouped). By default, table calculations are addressed from left to right. In this case, that makes the running total computed on the Segment dimension, leaving the Year of Order Date dimension as our partitioning field. I would prefer to swap those so that the running total is computed using the Year of Order Date field and grouped by the Segment dimension.

Fortunately, it is easy to change the direction of a table calculation by right-clicking a pill displaying a delta symbol, hovering over Compute Using, and choosing a different direction—or addressing field. Figure 11-9 shows the table after changing the addressing from Table (across) to Table (down).

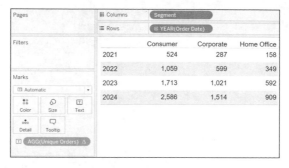

		Consumer	Corporate	Home Office
2021		524	287	158
2022		1,059	599	349
2023		1,713	1,021	592
2024		2,586	1,514	909

Figure 11-9. Running total table calculation addressed by Table (down) and partitioned by Segment

With the running total being computed from top to bottom for each segment, we see the desired result of where we ended up for each segment for the four years we've been in business.

This was a simple example because only one field is generating the rows, and one field is generating the columns. However, you can also compute (or address) table calculations with multiple fields. For more-complex calculated fields, choose the Add Table Calculation that appears after right-clicking a measure's pill or, if you have already added a quick table calculation, the Edit Table Calculation option.

Both options will give you more flexibility than the commonly used quick table calculations, and the calculation assistance interface will help you achieve the outcomes you are looking for. After adding a table calculation, you can always double-click a pill with a delta symbol to see the underlying formula generating the outcome on the view. Try copying and pasting these formulas into a calculated field dialog to look up their functions and learn what they're doing!

Level of Detail Calculations

Level of Detail calculations, or *LODs*, allow you to aggregate numbers at levels that are different from the default visualization level of detail. This can be handy should you not want a number influenced by extra dimensions added to a view and/or you want to use multiple levels of aggregation within a single view.

LODs are constructed with one of three statements:

- FIXED permanently sets the aggregation of a field based on the dimensions used in the calculated field.

- EXCLUDE ignores dimensions in the visualization level of detail, making the LOD less granular or more aggregated.

- INCLUDE adds dimensions to the visualization level of detail, making the LOD more granular or less aggregated.

We can better understand how each of these three LOD statements will impact computed results by reviewing Tableau's order of operations. Figure 11-10 shows the order of operations introduced in Chapter 10 with the different types of LOD functions highlighted.

Based on this order of operations, FIXED would be the best choice if we want to permanently fix the aggregation of a field and have it affected by nothing other than extract, data source, or context filters. If instead we would prefer that dimension filters process before our custom LOD aggregation is considered, we would use either an INCLUDE or EXCLUDE statement.

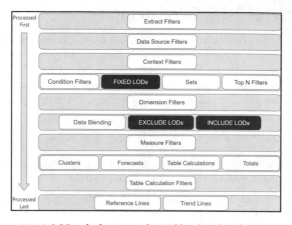

Figure 11-10. LOD calculations within Tableau's order of operations

In Figure 11-11, I have added the Category dimension to the bar chart created back in Figure 11-3.

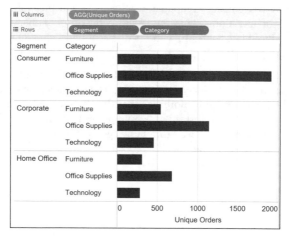

Figure 11-11. Unique Orders at the Segment and Category level of detail

For this view, Segment and Category are the visualization level of detail, so the Unique Orders or any measure I add to this view will be broken down by both Segment and Category. Let's say we also want to see Unique Orders at the Segment level, ignoring the Category breakdown so the second measure is less granular.

We can use an LOD to accomplish this. LOD calculations are constructed from the following:

- An open brace {
- A FIXED / INCLUDE / EXCLUDE statement
- The dimensions that you want addressed with the LOD statement, separated by commas if multiple dimensions are being addressed
- A colon punctuation mark :
- The aggregation of the field you want to compute the level of detail for (such as MIN, SUM); this can be left out if the field is already being aggregated within a calculated field
- An open parenthesis (
- The field you are computing the level of detail for
- A closed parenthesis)
- A closed brace }

To sum up unique orders while ignoring the Category dimension, create a calculated field with the formula {EXCLUDE [Category]: COUNTD([Order ID])}. Figure 11-12 shows the bar chart after adding my newly created Unique Orders Excluding Category measure to the Columns shelf. I've also added mark labels so we can quality-check the result.

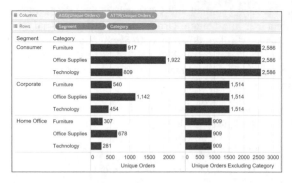

Figure 11-12. Unique Orders and Unique Orders Excluding Category bar chart

The left side of this chart is at the visualization level of detail, Segment and Category, while the right side is at the visualization level of detail *minus* the Category dimension (i.e., Segment only). We see the same number repeated at the Category level because our statement has instructed Tableau to ignore that additional breakdown.

In this case, we cannot add the unique orders from each category to see if the sum matches the result at the Segment level on the right because a unique ID from a segment can be in multiple categories. But we can easily quality-check this by removing the Category dimension from the Rows shelf. Doing so would make the visualization level of detail on the left match the LOD result on the right, and we would see the same numbers on both sides.

Lastly, you can combine the types of calculated fields covered in this chapter to create compound formulas. Say we want to compute a ratio that tells us the percent of unique orders by segment that contains at least one unique order per category. The formula would be [Unique Orders] / ATTR([Unique Orders Excluding Category]).

NOTE

The results of LOD calculations are considered nonaggregate, so they must be aggregated when used with other fields that are being aggregated in a calculated field. To avoid receiving an error message for using a combination of aggregated and nonaggregated measures, you can either repeat the aggregation used within the LOD statement as the aggregation or use the ATTR function (which returns the result of an expression when there is a single value). This provides the flexibility of aggregating a measure more than once!

By default, newly created calculated fields do not get any number formatting, but you can set the default number formatting by right-clicking a newly created calculated field and selecting Default Properties > Number Format. Because ratios should be presented as percentages, I have followed these steps with the Unique Orders Ratio calculated field to convert the calculation into a percentage with two decimal places

Figure 11-13 shows my aggregate calculated field, Unique Orders; Level of Detail calculation, Unique Orders Excluding Category; and the combination of the two, Unique Orders Ratio.

In this chapter, we have gone from not a single measure in the Sample – Superstore dataset related to orders to creating a complex formula to determine the ratio of unique orders between dimensions! As you can imagine, calculated fields are extremely flexible and can be constructed many ways. For example, I could have created the same Unique Orders Ratio by combining an aggregate calculated field with a table calculation instead of a Level of Detail calculation by using the formula [Unique Orders] / TOTAL([Unique Orders]).

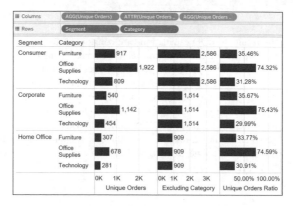

Segment	Category	Unique Orders	Excluding Category	Unique Orders Ratio
Consumer	Furniture	917	2,586	35.46%
	Office Supplies	1,922	2,586	74.32%
	Technology	809	2,586	31.28%
Corporate	Furniture	540	1,514	35.67%
	Office Supplies	1,142	1,514	75.43%
	Technology	454	1,514	29.99%
Home Office	Furniture	307	909	33.77%
	Office Supplies	678	909	74.59%
	Technology	281	909	30.91%

Figure 11-13. Combining types of calculated fields on a single view

This formula is simpler to write but has the drawback of making you ensure that the correct addressing and partitioning are in place, even if the table layout or fields being used should change.

TIP

To master calculated fields, I recommend browsing the data dictionary within the calculated field dialog, reverse-engineering table calculations by double-clicking pills you've added table calculations to, and most important, *practice* with real data!

CHAPTER 12

Parameters

Parameters are user-generated values that are not tied to a data source. These values can be used as inputs within calculated fields, reference lines, and/or filters. What makes this feature powerful is that after the author sets the limits of the values available in the parameter, the author and their users can change the value on-the-fly by using a *parameter control* or dashboard actions (discussed in Chapter 14).

This chapter shows you how to make a parameter, how to use dynamic parameters, and presents some popular use cases.

How to Make a Parameter

You can create a parameter by right-clicking any blank space on the Data pane or by left clicking the down-arrow in the top-right corner of the Data pane and choosing Create Parameter.

Although parameters don't show up in the underlying data, it helps to think of each parameter as a new column in a data source, with its single value appearing on every row. Since each parameter is a new column, you must assign it one of the six data types covered in Chapter 3. Figure 12-1 shows the Create Parameter dialog with the data type options.

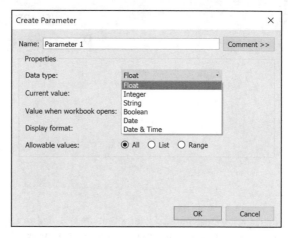

Figure 12-1. Create Parameter dialog

After setting the data type of the parameter, I recommend focusing on the "Allowable values" section of the dialog, where you can limit which values can be selected. There are three radio buttons to choose from:

All (the default)
> Allows the user to set any value as the value of the parameter

List
> Allows the author to set a list of options for the user

Range
> Allows the author to set a quantitative or date range with step sizes (i.e., multiples)

These radio buttons will automatically update to show you which options are relevant for the data type selected. For example, Range is not available with a data type of String because there is no quantitative or date range to set with text.

By default, a parameter's current value is the first or lowest allowable value. You can change the current value from within this dialog, but remember this is only the default value of the parameter and can be changed later by the user. You can also set the "Display format" from within this dialog, which is the equivalent of changing a calculated field's default number formatting. One last item you can change while creating or editing a parameter is "Value when workbook opens," covered in the next section.

Once you are ready to use a parameter, click the OK button to close this dialog. If this is the first parameter you have created in a workbook, you will see a new Parameters area appear in the Data pane. These parameter values work across data sources, so you will see the same Parameters area and parameters even when connecting to multiple data sources.

How to Use Dynamic Parameters

Beginning in version 2020.1, Tableau authors have the option to make parameters dynamic by either setting their current value or populating their allowable values when a workbook opens. The ability to automatically update parameter values improves both the author's and user's experience by keeping parameters up-to-date as underlying data is refreshed.

By default, a parameter is set to its current value, which is static. This means that it will not change until a user chooses a different allowable value. However, you can change this setting while either creating or editing a parameter with the "Value when workbook opens" option.

To use a field other than the parameter's static current value, you must have a Level of Detail calculated field using the FIXED expression that results in the same data type as the parameter. For example, if I want the current value of a date parameter to automatically update to the latest date in a dataset when the workbook opens, I would create a calculated field with the formula {FIXED: MAX([Date])}. After creating this calculated field, Figure 12-2 shows it available as a dynamic option.

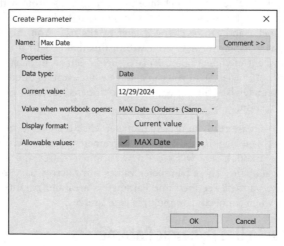

Figure 12-2. Dynamic current parameter values

You can also make a list of allowable values dynamic by clicking the "When workbook opens" radio button and choosing a field while creating a list. Figure 12-3 shows a new parameter with a data type of String and allowable values created from the Category dimension members.

The Category dimension from the Sample – Superstore dataset contains three dimension members. However, if the store began selling a category called Widgets and that dimension member appeared in the underlying data, these dynamic parameter settings would automatically update the list of allowable values the next time the Tableau workbook was opened!

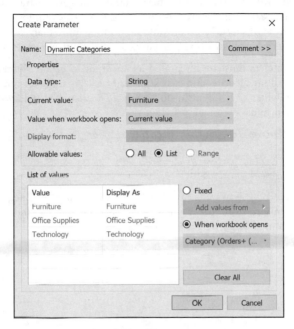

Figure 12-3. Dynamic list of allowable parameter values

Popular Use Cases

I often describe parameters as my Swiss Army knife because they are the solution to so many analytics and user experience questions that arise while authoring in Tableau. Parameters are the only feature that allow you and your users to store values that control the outcomes of other fields. This section shares a few useful ways to apply parameters.

Using a String for Dimension Member Highlighting and/or Filtering

Parameters are single values, so they do almost nothing on their own. If I were to put the Dynamic Categories parameter created earlier in Figure 12-3 onto the Rows or Columns shelf of any worksheet, Tableau would do nothing more than create a header labeled Furniture (the current value of the parameter).

Parameters must be integrated as an input to become useful. One of my favorite, and easiest, ways to use a parameter is as a highlighter or a filter. To do so, create a calculated field with this formula:

```
[Dimension you are highlighting or filtering]
=
[String parameter created with the same
dimension members]
```

Figure 12-4 shows this calculated field when using the Category dimension from the Sample – Superstore dataset and the Dynamic Categories parameter.

Figure 12-4. Category = Dynamic Categories row-level calculated field

This row-level calculated field creates a Boolean outcome. When the Category dimension member matches the Dynamic Categories allowable value, the outcome is True; otherwise, it is False. In Figure 12-5, I have placed this calculated field onto the Color property of the Marks card for the bar chart created in Chapter 5.

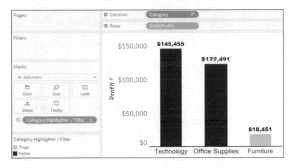

Figure 12-5. Bar chart highlighted by a parameter selection

Since Furniture is the current value of the parameter, the Furniture dimension member is the only calculation that results in an outcome of True—creating a highlight effect! Changing the value of the parameter to Technology or Office Supplies will move the highlight to the selection.

TIP

What's best about this technique is it can be rolled out across multiple worksheets. Placing the highlighter on the Marks card's Color property for any worksheet using the Category dimension will highlight the allowable value created in the single Dynamic Categories parameter.

The best way to change the value of a parameter is to right-click the parameter from the Data pane and select Show Parameter. This shows a control that can be changed by the author as well as by users of the workbook. Parameter values can also be changed by right-clicking the parameter from within the Data pane, choosing Edit, and making a different selection in the "Current value" drop-down.

The same calculated field 1 used to demonstrate the highlighting effect can also be used to filter views. If I were to drag the

Category Highlighter / Filter calculated field to the Filters shelf and choose True, the view would be filtered to only the current value of the parameter.

Using a Float for Scenario Playing

Parameters can also be used as numeric values within calculated fields. For the next example, we will do a basic what-if analysis that shows what would happen to our profit values by category if increased or decreased between 5% and 100%.

The first step is to create a parameter with a data type of Float (numbers with decimals). In Figure 12-6, I have created a parameter with a data type of Float, current value of 0, display format of Percentage with no decimal places, and an allowable range of values from –1 to 1 in multiples of 0.05.

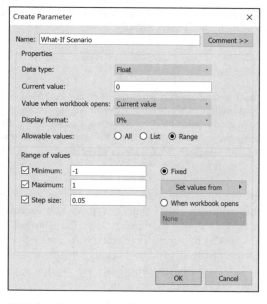

Figure 12-6. Creating a parameter for scenario playing

With these settings in place, the user can eventually choose any percentage value between minus 100% and positive 100% in increments of five percentage points. Again, this parameter alone does almost nothing; it is a single value currently equaling zero.

To make this single value useful, we must integrate it within a calculated field that will change the result of the calculation. In Figure 12-7, I've created a calculated field and written an aggregate calculation that will take the sum of the profit at the visualization level of detail multiplied by one plus the value of the What-If Scenario parameter.

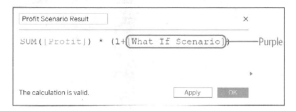

Figure 12-7. Profit Scenario Result calculated field

The purple color-coding indicates that the value will equal the current value of the What-If Scenario parameter, which we previously set up to allow choices from −1 to 1 in increments of 0.05. To quality-check the result, in Figure 12-8 I've added this field to the Rows shelf, shown the parameter by right-clicking the newly created What-If Scenario parameter and choosing Show Parameter, and changed the current value from 0% to 20%.

The values on the second row, Profit Scenario Result, are taking the original profit values by category and multiplying them by 1.2, showing us the Sample Superstore's profit values if they were to increase by 20%. With the confidence that we are computing the correct what-if scenario result, we can remove the original SUM(Profit) field from the Rows shelf and let the user control the profit values just by moving the parameter slider from left to right!

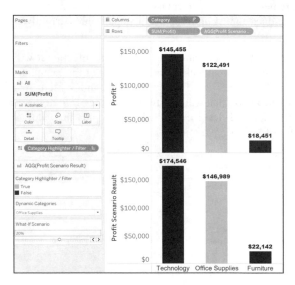

Figure 12-8. Quality-checking the Profit Scenario Result calculated field

Using a Dynamic Parameter for Date Filtering

One of the most useful ways to use a dynamic parameter is to automatically highlight or filter views based on the latest date in the dataset. This is easy to accomplish if you create the Max Date parameter shown previously in Figure 12-2. Once again, parameters are single values that become most useful when integrated within a calculated field.

For this tactic, we will use a function called DATETRUNC within a calculated field, which truncates a date at a specified date part. The syntax is DATETRUNC('Date Part',[Date]). This formula will roll up dates from the date used in the calculated field to the first day in the date part specified (day, week, month, quarter, year). For example, if I use a date part of month, and the date of January 16, then any other date in January will be assigned the value of January 1.

To filter the bar chart used throughout this chapter to the latest month in the dataset, I will create a calculated field that compares the Order Date field from the underlying data, truncated to the first day of the month, to the value of the Max Date parameter (the latest date in the dataset upon opening), also truncated to the first day of the month.

Here is the formula for this calculated field:

```
DATETRUNC('month',[Order Date])
=
DATETRUNC('month',[Max Date])
```

Figure 12-9 shows this formula within a calculated field with the data dictionary on the right showing the definition and syntax of the DATETRUNC function.

Figure 12-9. Date = Max Date Parameter calculated field

This calculated field creates a Boolean result; either the month of the Order Date field equals the month of the Max Date parameter or it doesn't. If I drag this field to the Filters shelf and choose to keep only the True result, the bar chart will be filtered to the latest month in the dataset, as shown in Figure 12-10.

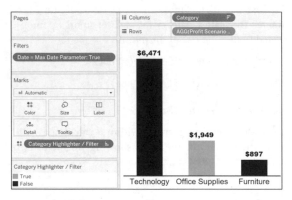

Figure 12-10. Profit Scenario Result by Category bar chart filtered to the latest month in the dataset

The benefit of using the dynamic Max Date parameter within the calculated field creating the filter is not only that the filter will automatically update to the show the latest month in the dataset upon the workbook opening, but also that you can show the Max Date parameter to allow the user to change which month is being displayed. Figure 12-11 is the bar chart after showing the Max Date parameter and changing the control to November 30.

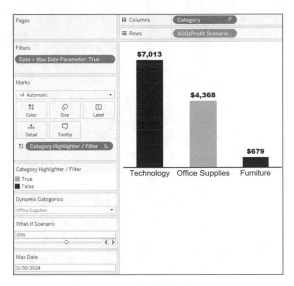

Figure 12-11. Bar chart being controlled by three parameters

The single Max Date parameter can control the month being displayed on any sheet using the Date = Max Date Parameter calculated field on the Filters shelf. We have just created an application that allows us and our workbook users to highlight the Category dimension member that is most relevant to them, do their own scenario analyses on the profit values, and filter the view to any month they choose!

CHAPTER 13

Sets

Sets are Boolean fields that classify dimension members as either *In* or *Out*. The ability to isolate dimension members into sets allows the author to treat them in different ways. This chapter shows you two ways to make sets. You'll then learn how to use them as a filter, as a dimension, within calculated fields, and as a highlighter.

How to Create Sets

For a use case, let's return to the scatter plot created in Chapter 9 that revealed we have 10 states that are generating below $0 in average profit. We can use sets to isolate these dimension members for further investigation.

In Figure 13-1, I have returned to the scatter plot worksheet, this time changing the mark type to Circle instead of Shape and began creating a set. The easiest way to create a set is to draw a box around any dimension members on a chart, hover over any of the selected dimension members, click the Set icon, and choose Create Set.

This will open a dialog where you can give the set a name and refine the dimension members included (or optionally excluded) in the set, as shown in Figure 13-2.

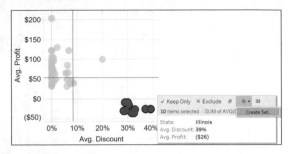

Figure 13-1. Creating a static set

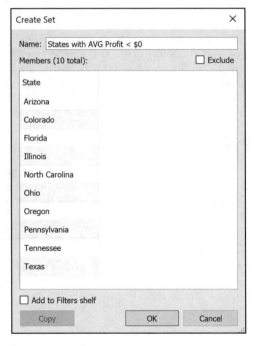

Figure 13-2. Create Set dialog

After clicking the OK button, you will see a new field appear along with other dimensions on the Data pane. If you are using a version of Tableau Desktop prior to 2020.2, you will see any set you create appear in its own Sets area of the Data pane. In either case, sets are identified with a Venn diagram icon preceding them on the Data pane.

This first method of creating a set allows us to visually select exactly which dimension members are included or excluded from the set, but it comes with the drawback of being *static*. This means that the dimension members in the set will be stuck that way forever until we manually add or remove additional members. This can be problematic when underlying data refreshes because dimension members may no longer meet the original criteria for being part of the set (i.e., one of the states turns profitable).

If you would prefer to create a dynamic set that automatically reclassifies dimension members as In or Out as underlying data refreshes, from within the Data pane, right-click the dimension from which you want to create the set and select Create > Set. This opens a dialog that is similar to the dimension filter created in Chapter 10, where you can manually choose dimension members on the General tab, set criteria on the Condition tab, or define a top or bottom *N* on the Top tab.

In Figure 13-3, I have started creating a set from the State dimension, navigated to the Condition tab, and entered a formula that will classify dimension members with average profit values of less than zero into the set.

Figure 13-3. Creating a dynamic set

With the criterion I've established for this set, Tableau will look at the State level of detail and classify any states with average profit values less than zero as In the set, and any states with average profit values greater than or equal to zero as Out of the set. Because of Tableau's order of operations, sets are established before dimension and measure filters, meaning, by default, the set classification of dimension members won't be affected should you add dimension and/or measure filters to the Filters shelf. If you prefer to have a dimension filter compute before a set, you can add the dimension filter to context to move it up in the order of operations, as discussed in Chapter 10.

Currently, the static set created with the first approach and dynamic set created with the second approach will produce the same result because the same 10 states are in both sets. The difference with the second approach is that if a state's average profit values rise above zero as data is updated and/or a state that was previously profitable dips below zero, Tableau will automatically reclassify the dimension members for us!

Practical Use Cases

Sets are a powerful way to segment the dimension members in your dataset for deeper analysis. Here are just a few uses of this feature.

Sets as a Filter

Sets can filter marks on a view just like other dimensions by dragging them to the Filters shelf. With sets, the default behavior is for Tableau to keep dimension members that are *in* the set. In Figure 13-4, I have dragged the "States with AVG Profit < 0" set to the Filters shelf of the scatter plot, and Tableau instantly filtered the view to the 10 unprofitable dimension members.

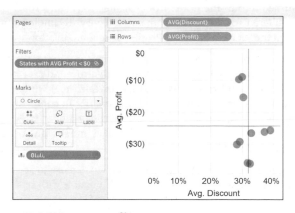

Figure 13-4. Using a set as a filter

This is an alternative way to filter dimension members using quantitative thresholds, as we did with the measure filter in Chapter 10 (Figure 10-2). The difference is this filter is Boolean, grouping every dimension member into one of two outcomes: In or Out.

If you would prefer the option to view those dimension members *outside* the set and/or want to see both outcomes at the same time, right-click the set on the Filters shelf and choose Show In/Out of the Set. This will open a filter dialog for defining more-specific criteria.

Lastly, if you want you and your user to have one-click access to changing the filter to show members in the set, out of the set, or both, right-click the set on the Filters shelf and choose Show Filter.

Sets as a Dimension

Sets can also be used as a dimension by dragging them to either the Rows shelf or Columns shelf. In Figure 13-5, I have returned to our line graph from Chapter 10 (Figure 10-4) that was filtered to our most profitable category, Technology, and placed the "States with AVG Profit < 0" set onto the Rows shelf.

This has created two rows, showing me the quarterly profit trend for the 10 states in the set on the first row and everything else on a second row. This chart has revealed that while most states were enjoying their second-best quarter in company history, the 10 unprofitable states had their worst quarter ever. It also looks like the 10 unprofitable states missed out on the recent holiday spike.

We now have at least two tangible paths to explore to see if we can turn around this profit story—made possible with sets!

Figure 13-5. Using a set as a dimension

Sets within Calculated Fields

Sets can be used to write calculated fields more efficiently. For example, instead of coding IF AVG([Profit]) < 0 THEN, we can write IF [Set] THEN. When using sets within calculated fields, Tableau applies the logic being used to members *in* the set.

Although typing out IF AVG([Profit]) < 0 THEN will aggregate values at the visualization level of detail, IF [Set] THEN will always apply the criteria at the level of detail specified within the set. This can make it easier to understand the logic within a calculated field. Not only that, but sets are also Boolean, which is the easiest data type for Tableau to process.

In Figure 13-6, I have created a calculated field to visualize the result if we were able to raise the average profit value of our unprofitable states by $15.

```
Unprofitable States + 15                                    ×

IF ATTR([States with AVG Profit < $0])
THEN AVG([Profit]) + 15
ELSE AVG([Profit])
END



The calculation is valid.              Apply      OK
```

Figure 13-6. Using a set within a calculated field

This formula will add $15 to the average profit values of members in the set while returning the actual profit values for members outside the set.

TIP

To ensure that the result of this calculated field is properly aggregated, I have wrapped the States with AVG Profit < 0 set in the ATTR function. This function returns the value of the expression as long as there is a single value within it, which is the case here with our set returning the value of In. The ATTR function is handy when combining sets, dates, and/or dimensions containing single members with measures because it counts as an aggregation. Without the ATTR function being applied to the set in this case, I would get an error message indicating I cannot use a mix of aggregate and nonaggregate values.

If I replace the AVG(Profit) field on the scatter plot shown in Figure 13-1 with the newly created Unprofitable States + 15 calculated field, I can visualize the result, as shown in Figure 13-7.

It looks like adding $15 to the average profit of our 10 unprofitable states would turn two of them profitable, with a third close to turning positive. In this example, I hardcoded the addition of $15, but you could parameterize this as described in Chapter 12 for a more dynamic analysis.

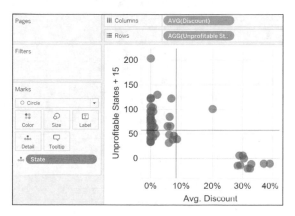

Figure 13-7. AVG(Discount) by Unprofitable States + 15 scatter plot

Sets as a Highlighter

Sets can be used as a highlighter by dragging and dropping them to the Color property on the Marks card. Doing so will color all dimension members in the set one color, and every dimension member outside the set a second color. In Figure 13-8, I have added the "States with AVG Profit < 0" set to the scatter plot to communicate which states are in the set, and thus having $15 added to their average profit values.

Just as we used parameters as a highlighter in Chapter 12, this single set can be used to color dimension members across multiple worksheets. To make this technique even more effective, you can edit the aliases of the colors by right-clicking either In or Out on the color legend and choosing Edit Alias. In this case, I might edit the In alias to States with AVG Profit < 0 or What-If Scenario Applied, and the Out alias to States with AVG Profit > 0 or Actuals.

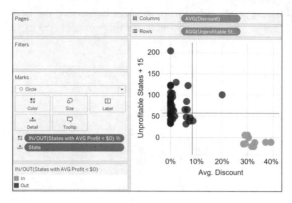

Figure 13-8. Using a set as a highlighter

NOTE

Tableau introduced the *set control* in version 2020.2, which allows you to add and remove dimension members from a set just as you would with a filter that is being shown on a view. To add a set control to a view, the set must be created with the dialog shown in Figure 13-3 and be used somewhere on the view. If you have met these criteria, you can add a set control by right-clicking the set from within the Data pane and choosing Show Set.

Equipped with the skills to create some of the most effective chart types and apply some of the most essential technical features of Tableau Desktop, you are ready to tie everything together by creating dashboards!

CHAPTER 14

Dashboards and Distribution

Up to this point in the book, all examples have been built and showcased on individual worksheets. While this provides value, particularly for narrowly focused analyses or answering ad hoc questions of your data, these individual views become even more powerful when combined using *dashboards*.

Tableau Desktop provides this ability via its Dashboard interface, allowing authors to view various aspects of the data in context of each other and create flexible user experiences to help analysts find insights. This chapter shows you how to make a dashboard in Tableau Desktop, discusses aspects of the Dashboard interface, and provides several choices for distributing completed dashboards.

The Dashboard Pane

To create a dashboard in Tableau Desktop, either click the second-to-last tab at the bottom of the Authoring interface or navigate to Dashboard > New Dashboard in the top menu. This opens a new interface containing the Dashboard and Layout panes instead of the Authoring interface's Data and Analytics panes.

Choosing the Layout and Size of a Dashboard

The first options you see at the top of the Dashboard pane control the layout and size of the dashboard. When Default is selected as the layout, the dashboard will be sized by the dimensions selected in the Size drop-down menu. Every dashboard created in Tableau also comes with a preset Phone layout that will automatically adjust the size and location of dashboard objects when a mobile device is being used to view dashboards on Tableau Server, Tableau Online, or Tableau Public.

TIP

If you prefer that Tableau not automatically resize a dashboard when it is being viewed on a phone, hover your mouse pointer over the Phone layout, click the ellipsis that appears, and choose Delete Layout. Alternatively, you can click Dashboard in the top menu and deselect Add Phone Layouts to New Dashboards. You also have the option to create additional layouts by clicking the Device Preview button. In this area, you can sift through multiple device types and models to see how your dashboard will look when being viewed on various browser sizes. To save one of these layouts and have Tableau automatically serve the best dashboard layout for the user, click the Add Layout button in the top right-corner of Device Preview mode.

In the Size drop-down, authors can set the default layout of the dashboard, down to the pixel, by using the "Fixed size" option, or have the dashboard automatically resize to fill any screen it is displayed on by using the Automatic option. As shown in Figure 14-1, the default is a preset fixed size called Desktop Browser.

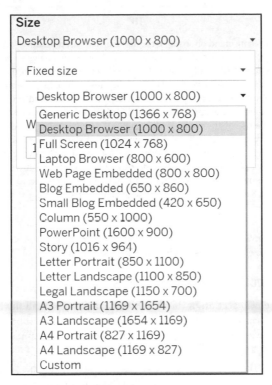

Figure 14-1. Dashboard dimension presets

The first number in parentheses sets the dashboard's width in pixels, and the second number sets its height. When using fixed sizes, the dashboard will have the same dimensions regardless of the display's screen size or resolution.

Both the fixed and automatic options have pros and cons. Automatic is more practical if stakeholders will be viewing dashboards across multiple devices, whereas Fixed leads to more-precise designs.

I recommend choosing a dashboard size based on how you plan to distribute the dashboard. Doing an analysis for yourself that only you will see? Try Automatic size to use all available screen space on the device you are using. Know your colleague always views your dashboard on a tablet? Use a smaller dashboard footprint that can optimize the use of the reduced real estate. If you just can't decide, two of my favorites are the preset fixed sizes: PowerPoint and Letter Landscape. With the former, I can copy and paste entire dashboards and know they will fit perfectly on a PowerPoint slide, while the latter can be printed and fit an 8.5 × 11 piece of paper in a horizontal orientation.

For now, I have set the dashboard dimensions to a custom, fixed size of 400 pixels wide by 800 pixels high.

Dashboard Sheets and Objects

In the next section of the Dashboard pane, you see all the individual worksheets that are available to add to the dashboard. If you have been following along with this book's examples, you will see a bar chart, line graph, and scatter plot.

You can rename these sheets at any time by either right-clicking them on the Dashboard pane and choosing Rename Sheet, or double-clicking the original tab at the bottom of the screen and typing over what is there by default. As shown in Figure 14-2, Tableau also provides a thumbnail preview of the sheet's content to help ensure that you are choosing the intended worksheet to add to the dashboard.

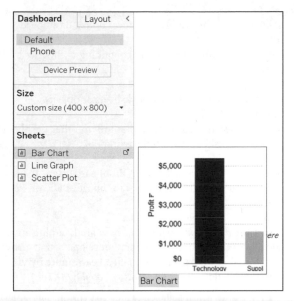

Figure 14-2. Choosing a sheet to add to a dashboard

In addition to worksheets, authors can also add dashboard objects to enhance the layout, design, and user experience of dashboards. In the Objects section of the Dashboard pane, authors can add the following:

Horizontal

Short for *Horizontal Layout Container*, this option allows you to group one or more worksheets and/or dashboard objects in a landscape orientation. When worksheets or objects are in the same container, they can be moved and formatted in unison.

Vertical

This is also a layout container, but the worksheets or objects placed within it will be in a portrait orientation.

Text

Opens a word processor for adding custom text.

Image
> Allows the author to place pictures onto a dashboard.

Web Page
> Creates an embedded iframe containing a URL set by the author.

Blank
> Adds whitespace between worksheets or objects.

Navigation
> Can be used to add buttons that link to other dashboards and/or worksheets within the workbook.

Download
> Provides one-click access for dashboard users to download the dashboard as a crosstab, image, PDF, or Power-Point file.

Extension
> Short for *dashboard extension*, these are like plug-ins created by Tableau and third-party developers that provide additional dashboard functionality. Learn more by visiting Tableau's Extension Gallery (*https://oreil.ly/4XTvL*).

These features are completely optional and should be based on the experience you want to provide to your dashboard users. Simple dashboards may use a single layout container holding two worksheets, while more-complex dashboards may utilize every one of these objects. Whatever the case, when you are ready to add a worksheet or object to a dashboard, you must select whether it is tiled or floating.

Tiled, Floating, and Hybrid Objects

By default, any worksheet added to a dashboard will be *tiled*. I think of this setting as tiling a floor: each tile fills its allotted space, and (hopefully!) they all line up with no gaps between them.

As you add objects to a dashboard, Tableau displays gray shading indicating where the object will be placed. When adding objects as tiled, the gray shading will fill entire dashboard areas, leaving no gaps between objects.

In Figure 14-3, I have added the bar chart from Chapter 12 and the scatter plot from Chapter 13 as tiled worksheets.

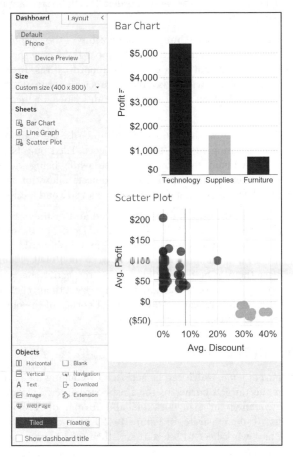

Figure 14-3. Dashboard containing two tiled worksheets

When adding worksheets to a dashboard, any legends, filters, and parameters being shown on the worksheet will automatically appear on the dashboard as tiled objects within a container. These can optionally be removed by clicking within the object you want to remove, and then clicking the X in the top-right corner of the gray border that appears around selected objects.

If you click the Floating button at the bottom of the Dashboard pane before adding an object to a dashboard, the gray shading will no longer fill full areas of the dashboard canvas. Instead, any *floating* object will be layered at precise coordinates and can be controlled on the Layout pane described in the next section.

As with fixed- and automatic-sized dashboards, there are pros and cons to using tiled or floating objects. Tiled objects will resize to maintain their relational size while being viewed across different devices, and floating objects allow for more precision because you can control their exact size and location.

You also have the option to use both tiled and floating objects at the same time, which I call *hybrid objects*. For example, instead of deleting unwanted legends from a dashboard, I may convert them to floating so they float over tiled objects and I can place them in better relation to their respective sheets. To convert objects between tiled and floating, select them, click the down arrow that appears in the top-right corner of the object, and select or deselect Floating.

The Layout Pane

The *Layout pane*, which can be accessed by clicking the Layout tab in the top-left corner of the Dashboard interface, can be used to refine the size, location, and format of dashboard objects. To demonstrate, in Figure 14-4 I have clicked on the Bar Chart worksheet to select it and then clicked the Layout pane displayed.

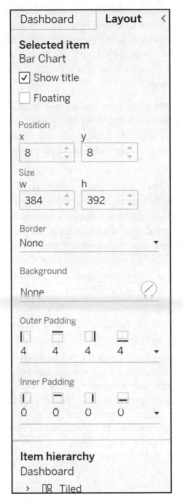

Figure 14-4. The Layout pane

The first two options, "Show title" and Floating, allow you to choose whether a worksheet's title is displayed and convert a worksheet from tiled to floating, respectively. Both options can also be accessed by selecting a worksheet on the dashboard and then clicking the down arrow that appears in the top-right corner of the worksheet.

The Position settings show the x and y coordinates of the object, and the Size settings show the object's width and height, both in terms of pixels. Although you can see these settings for tiled objects, they can be changed only manually for floating objects.

Farther down on the Layout pane, you have the option to add a border and/or background color to the selected object. Clicking the Border drop-down opens options for choosing the format, weight, and color of a border. Clicking the Background Color drop-down allows you to choose from many preset colors, recently used colors, or custom colors. Within the Background Color drop-down, you can also set the transparency of a selected color by moving the Opacity slider.

NOTE

Each worksheet has a white background that overrides the background color set on the Layout pane. If you prefer a worksheet with no background color—which is particularly useful for floating objects that are layered on top of one another—right-click anywhere in the worksheet and choose Format, navigate to the Shading tab of options, and set the Worksheet shading to None.

The remaining formatting options, Outer Padding and Inner Padding, allow you to add pixels of whitespace around the outside or inside of an object, respectively. By default, every object has four pixels of outer padding on all sides. Prior to these padding features being introduced on the Layout pane, the only way to create whitespace between tiled objects was to add Blank dashboard objects, described in the "Dashboard Sheets and Objects" section of this chapter.

The final feature of the Layout pane, Item Hierarchy, shows you which objects are on the dashboard and their layer order. I've explained how to select dashboard objects by clicking them from within the dashboard, but you can also select dashboard objects by clicking their name within this hierarchy. You can also reorder the layers of floating objects by clicking them from within this hierarchy and dragging them up or down in the list.

Dashboard Actions

Dashboard actions are a key feature for designing user experiences because they allow you to pass values by selecting them on worksheets. For example, I can add a dashboard action that filters every worksheet on a dashboard to the same dimension member when a user clicks the dimension member on one of the sheets. Dashboard actions can also be used to highlight values, navigate users to external URLs, navigate users to different worksheets, change parameter values, or change set values.

To add a dashboard action, click Dashboard in the top menu and choose Actions. In the Actions dialog that opens, click the Add Action button and choose from one of the six types of dashboard actions, shown in Figure 14-5.

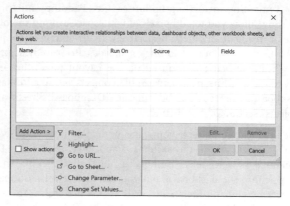

Figure 14-5. Actions dialog for adding, editing, or deleting a dashboard action

These options, which are intuitively named, do the following:

Filter

Has selected dimension members act as a filter

Highlight

Highlights selected dimension members

Go to URL

Navigates users to an external URL

Go to Sheet

Navigates users to a different sheet within the workbook

Change Parameter

Changes the current value of a parameter

Change Set Values

Changes the dimension members included in a set

As an example, let's say I want my user to be able to click a category on my dashboard's Profit by Category bar chart in order to filter the scatter plot to the selected dimension member. This would require a Filter dashboard action, because I'm using a sheet as a filter. Therefore, I choose Filter from the Actions dialog, which opens the interface shown in Figure 14-6.

The first thing you should do in this dialog is give the action an intuitive name that will help you find it later if you are using multiple dashboard actions.

In the first section, Source Sheets, you are setting the origin of the action. In my use case, I am wanting dimension members selected on my bar chart to filter the scatter plot, so Bar Chart is my source sheet.

On the right side of this dialog, you have the option to have the action execute upon various interactions. By default, the action will run on Menu, which appears as a link in a tooltip when a user hovers over a dimension member on a source sheet. You can also have the action execute immediately when a user hovers over a dimension member on a source sheet. For our use case, I want the filter to execute when a user selects, or clicks, a dimension member, so I choose Select.

In the next section of the dialog, you can choose the Target Sheets of the action, or in this case, the sheets that will be filtered after a selection is made in the source sheet. To the right of this section, you can choose what happens when an action is cleared, which you can do when using a Select action by clicking the Escape key (when using Tableau Desktop), clicking the selection a second time, or clicking whitespace within a dashboard.

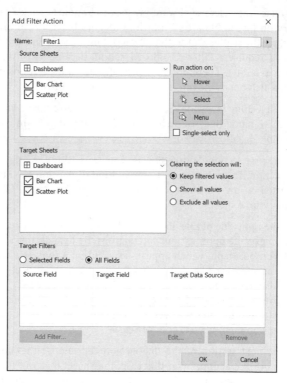

Figure 14-6. Add Filter Action dialog

The last option within the Add Filter Action dialog allows you to refine the fields that will be passed as part of the action. By default, this is set to All Fields and will pass all dimension members associated with the selection. In the current use case, the bar chart contains only one dimension, so I can leave this setting in place, and my new action is complete (Figure 14-7).

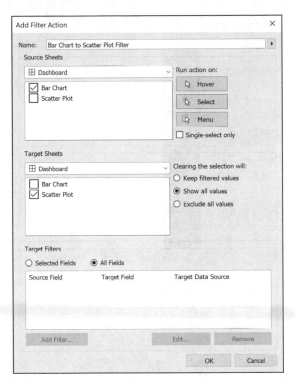

Figure 14-7. Filter dashboard action that will filter the scatter plot based on the dimension member(s) selected in the bar chart

With these settings in place, clicking a category in the bar chart will filter the scatter plot to the selected category. Figure 14-8 shows my dashboard after clicking the Technology category on the bar chart.

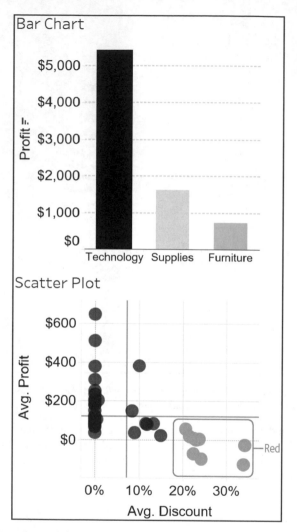

Figure 14-8. Filter dashboard action in use

The red circles are from our practical application of using sets as a highlighter (demonstrated in Chapter 13) and are indicating which states are below $0 in average profit overall. By filtering the scatter plot to the Technology category, I can see that six of the ten unprofitable states overall have positive average profit values within Technology. I also noticed the scale of the y-axis changed from –$50 to $200, as shown before in Figure 14-3, to –$100 to over $600, indicating the Technology category has more potential for profit.

These insights and user experience are made possible with dashboard actions! With dashboard actions, authors have to code the user experience only once, and then users can explore a dashboard to find what is relevant to them. Interactions like these work within Tableau Desktop, Tableau Reader, Tableau Public, Tableau Online, and Tableau Server.

Distributing Dashboards

After building a dashboard, you have the option to get it into the hands of your stakeholders in several ways, which are covered in this section.

Tableau Server or Tableau Online

If you or your company are using Tableau Server or Tableau Online in addition to your Tableau Desktop license, you can publish both workbooks and data sources for other users in your organization. This is the most secure, enterprise-level option for distributing views built in Tableau Desktop.

To publish a workbook, click Server > Sign In from the top menu. After signing into either Tableau Server or Tableau Online, click Server in the top menu again, and then Publish Workbook. Figure 14-9 shows the options that appear while publishing a workbook.

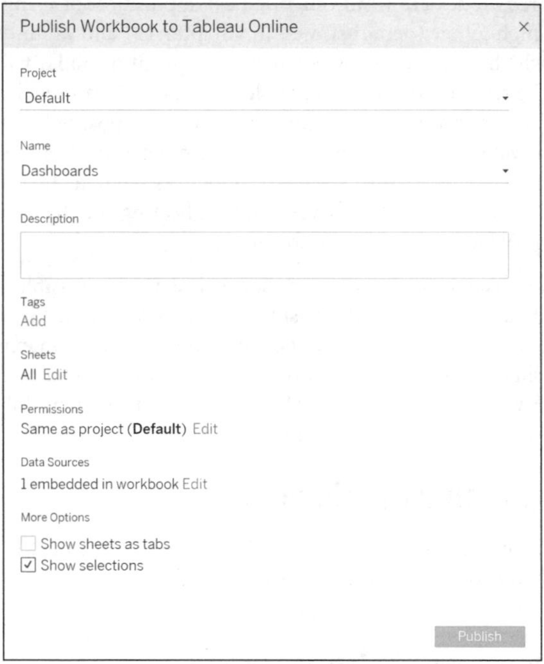

Figure 14-9. Publishing a workbook to Tableau Online

After clicking the Publish button, the workbook will be published and saved where users can access your work via a web browser. All the interaction you enabled—including filters, parameters, and dashboard actions—carries over to the shared version!

Tableau Public

Another option for sharing a workbook with all interactive features intact is Tableau Public. To save a workbook to Tableau Public, you first must sign up for a free Tableau Public account (*https://oreil.ly/mLWgr*). Then from the top menu, choose Server > Tableau Public > Save to Tableau Public As.

After signing in, you will be prompted to give the workbook a name, and it will be saved to Tableau Public. Remember that anything saved to Tableau Public can be found by anybody on the web. This makes it an unsuitable option for confidential business data, but it is still a great place to practice, share public data, and learn from others.

Tableau Packaged Workbook

Tableau has a free Tableau Reader product that allows anybody with the program to view and interact with local (unpublished) versions of your workbook. This acts much like a PDF reader, where you can save a Word document, for example, as a PDF. Then you can send the PDF to somebody who can view the file even if they don't have a license to Microsoft Word.

To save a workbook you've built in Tableau Desktop for somebody to view and interact with using Tableau Reader, you must save the file as a packaged workbook in one of two ways. First, from the top menu, you can choose File > Save As and then change the "Save as type" drop-down to Tableau Packaged Workbook. You can also choose File > Export Packaged Workbook.

Both options will save the workbook with the file extension *.twbx*, indicating it is a packaged workbook containing both the views and the data being used to create the views. Packaged workbooks can then be emailed to stakeholders who can open them with the Reader product. This is a good option for allowing users to interact with a workbook, but this process cannot be automated and is less secure because files can be distributed outside company walls.

PDF

Any worksheet, dashboard, or entire workbook can be printed to PDF by choosing File > Print to PDF. Figure 14-10 shows the various options for printing to PDF.

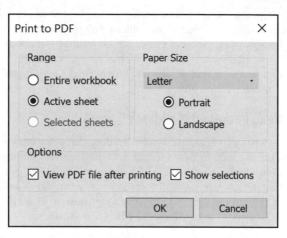

Figure 14-10. Print to PDF dialog

TIP

Although not as secure of an option as publishing an interactive version to Tableau Server or Tableau Online—because, again, this file can potentially be emailed outside company walls—I find PDFs are a great way to drive adoption of your analytics work. It is much easier to print out a hard copy of a dashboard and put it on somebody's desk than it is to explain how to access it via a browser.

PowerPoint

Like the Print to PDF option, any worksheet, dashboard, or entire workbook can be saved as a PowerPoint file by choosing File > Export as PowerPoint. Figure 14-11 shows the three options available within the Export PowerPoint dialog, accessed from the dashboard view we have been using in this chapter.

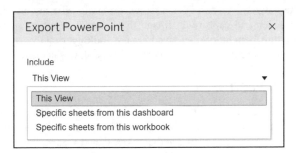

Figure 14-11. Export PowerPoint options from within a dashboard view

When exporting to PowerPoint from within a dashboard view, you can choose to export the current view; specific sheets within the dashboard; or specific sheets from within the workbook, whether or not they are included in the dashboard. When you select either "Specific sheets from this dashboard" or "Specific sheets from this workbook," thumbnail images of sheets will appear that you can choose to include in the exported PowerPoint file.

You can also export to PowerPoint from within an individual worksheet view, but you will see only the options to export "This View" or "Specific sheets from this workbook."

After saving an export, Tableau will create a PowerPoint document containing a cover slide with the title and date of export as well as one slide per view you chose to export.

Images

If none of the preceding options fits your needs, remember that you can always just share an image of a worksheet or dashboard. To export an entire dashboard as an image, choose Dashboard > Export Image from the top menu to export individual worksheets, select a worksheet by clicking it from within a dashboard or navigating to its respective tab, and then choose Worksheet > Export > Image.

Alternatively, you can open a screen-grabbing program on your computer and capture an image that way. This option comes with the benefit of the saved image looking exactly as you intended and is how every image in this book was created!

Conclusion

This book has provided a strong foundation for your visual analytics journey with Tableau, but this is just the beginning. Tableau Desktop is software that takes a day to learn, but a lifetime to master. I'm still picking up tricks after more than a decade of using the tool!

If you are looking for more chart-type tutorials, an introduction to strategy and storytelling, and "201-level" techniques, I recommend reading my first Tableau book, *Practical Tableau: 100 Tips, Tutorials, and Strategies from a Tableau Zen Master*, next. Once you are ready to level up and try some advanced chart types and techniques, move on to my second Tableau book, *Innovative Tableau: 100 More Tips, Tutorials, and Strategies*.

This is not to mention countless other resources available to enhance your learning. One of the strongest aspects of Tableau is its passionate, selfless community that often acts as a support system to learn from, inspire one another, and/or utilize as built-in peer review for your work. Whether your continued learning path takes you to blogs, in-person training events, video tutorials, or community programs to help you practice, know that many people are out there cheering you on as you take on the exciting prospect of changing the world with data.

Index

About the Author

Ryan Sleeper is founder and principal at Playfair Data and has consulted with many of the world's best-known brands. He is author of the books *Practical Tableau* (O'Reilly 2018) and *Innovative Tableau* (O'Reilly 2020), and has shared his data visualization strategies worldwide, including speaking engagements in London, Tokyo, Toronto, and Singapore. Ryan's work in Tableau has earned him the titles of Tableau Zen Master, Tableau Global Iron Viz Champion, and Tableau Public Visualization of the Year author.

Colophon

The bird on the cover of *Tableau Desktop Pocket Reference* is a western meadowlark (*Sturnella neglecta*). Western meadowlarks live in western and central North American grasslands, fields, prairies, and meadows. Their song distinguishes them from eastern meadowlarks.

Meadowlarks have bright yellow necks and bellies, with a black V neckline. Their top and tail feathers are white and brown. Adults are 6–10 inches long, weigh 3–4 ounces, and have a wingspan of about 16 inches. They forage for insects and seeds in the grass and build their nests on the ground as well. Western meadowlark eggs are white with purple and brown spots.

The western meadowlark has some protected habitat and the population is decreasing. Many of the animals on O'Reilly covers are endangered; all of them are important to the world.

The cover illustration is by Karen Montgomery. The cover fonts are Gilroy Semibold and Guardian Sans. The text font is Adobe Minion Pro; the heading font is Adobe Myriad Condensed; and the code font is Dalton Maag's Ubuntu Mono.